MY STORY or How I Managed to Survive Fifty-Six Years Teaching High School

DON HUMPHREY

BALBOA.
PRESS
A DIVISION OF HAY HOUSE

Balboa Press books may be ordered through booksellers or by contacting:

Balboa Press
A Division of Hay House
1663 Liberty Drive
Bloomington, IN 47403
www.balboapress.com.au
1 (877) 407-4847

Print information available on the last page.

ISBN: 978-1-5043-1619-4 (sc)
ISBN: 978-1-5043-1620-0 (e)

Balboa Press rev. date: 12/19/2018

I want to dedicate this book to the memory of my wife. Without her support and dedication, I never could have achieved the goals I had set out to do. She allowed me the time to pursue my aims, often pushing aside her ambitions to support mine. I owe all my successes to her.

Contents

Introduction

I began teaching in 1955 and finally called it quits in 2010, when I was approaching my seventy-seventh birthday. This book is my story.

When I was in fifth year (grade 11), our class was taken to do IQ tests. The scores were used to allocate grades for our Leaving Certificate. I don't remember my score, but I do remember the recommendation: I should consider a career as a microbiologist.

At the end of 1950, as a school student, I attended a cadet camp for promotion to cadet lieutenant. I got sick the first day and was taken to hospital, suffering kidney stones. I was in hospital for over a month before being discharged. I started school some weeks into the school year. (In Australia, the school year begins in January and ends in December.) I believe that this initial disruption to the year contributed to a rather poor result in the final exam. I repeated the final year in 1951. My subjects for the second time at the Leaving Certificate were English, Physics honours, Chemistry honours, Mathematics I honours, and Mathematics II. I got second class honours in Physics and Chemistry, A's in Mathematics I and II, and a B in English. These grades were enough to secure an Exihibition (a state scholarship), which would pay my university fees.

When we did the Leaving Certificate, we applied for scholarships. One of the scholarships I applied for was a State Public Service scholarship to become a microbiologist. I was awarded the scholarship, along with a Commonwealth scholarship and a Teachers College scholarship. The scholarship I was awarded from the Public Service was to train as a meteorologist.

I thought long and hard about that. The Commonwealth scholarship was okay. It paid all the university fees, but teaching versus weather forecasting created a dilemma. If I chose meteorology, I would be required to also choose geography as a subject. I had not studied any geography since primary school. Choosing teaching allowed me greater freedom. After much thought and a reminder from the Public Service that the time to accept was running out, I opted for the teaching scholarship. This placed me under a bond, which meant that I had to teach for at least three years or pay back the university fees.

Part of the deal with the teaching scholarship was that there was a living allowance. It amounted to a princely sum of three pounds (six dollars) a week. I gave Mum two pounds and got a couple of part-time jobs. The *Daily Mirror,* a popular evening newspaper gave me fifteen shillings ($1.50) to accompany a casual sports writer to a soccer or cricket match, depending on the season. The writer would write his copy on small sheets of note paper. I would then ring the phone number of the *Daily Mirror* and read the copy to the sports department, where it would be typed ready for the next edition of the Saturday afternoon newspaper. One of the typists was the Australian champion typist. It was a pleasure to dictate to her. On two occasions, the sports writer was ill and couldn't attend the game. It was then up to me.

My other job was to work as a shop assistant in a men's store in Hurstville, a neighbouring suburb. I was not much of a shop assistant, not having the courage to "suggest sell." If someone wanted to buy something, that was okay. I would wrap it up and take the cash and deal with it, but it never occurred to me that I could possibly sell something else from my department, which was men's underwear and socks. Women would come in and ask for underwear. I would always ask what size their husband wore. This worked out okay until one lady told me that the item was for herself. I never reached the magic twenty-five pounds' worth of sales. At that level, I would have received a bonus. I did get into trouble once for using too much wrapping paper.

Older readers may recall the system used in this store where money and the invoice were put into a container which was sent via overhead wires to a central cashier, who would verify the invoice and send it back to the shop assistant, together with any change.

I opted to do a Science degree at university, choosing Senior Physics, Chemistry, Mathematics, and Botany as my first-year studies. My results at the end of the year were okay. I passed all my subjects. I then had to respond to my compulsory call-up to do National Service. Whereas most young men could choose the army, navy, or air force, university students had to go into the army for their basic training. They then had to spend the remainder of three years in the Citizens Military Force. The university starting date for all students entering second year, even women, was postponed allowing for this. I chose Senior Physics II, Mathematics II, and Statistics. At the end of the year, I passed Statistics with posts in Physics and Maths but ended up failing. The rule in the Science degree was that you had to pass all subjects to continue. This meant that the scholarship was suspended until I passed the year or went to Teachers College. My father volunteered to pay my fees to repeat the year, but I opted to go to Teachers College, where my tuition was paid for and I would still receive an allowance. My father had three others to bring up and had already sacrificed much for me.

At Teachers College, I was placed in a section called "Returned University – Science/Maths." There was also a similar section for Arts. There we did the academic subjects and teaching methods and participated in practice sessions in public schools. This year was okay, and I passed out at the end of the year as a two-year trained assistant teacher. I had to complete three satisfactory years of teaching for the final certificate to be issued. I was confined to teaching classes from first to third year (grade 7–9). Years later, regulations were changed so that a two-year trained teacher could become a three-year trained teacher (with a salary rise) after completing a required number of university subjects. I went through that phase as I studied for a degree through distance education. Eventually, I got my degree and was eligible to become a graduate assistant. At this stage, I was already a special master (non-graduate) in charge of Science so, with the degree, I became a Science master.

After inspection, I was placed on List 3, which made me eligible to apply to become a deputy principal. Promotion beyond that to principal required another inspection to get onto List 4.

After applying for a position as deputy principal of a school several years in succession, my number finally came up, and I was finally appointed. During the time I was a deputy principal, I was inspected twice for promotion to principal but failed each time. In all fairness, I was not the person the inspectors were looking for. More of this later.

Later, principals were selected after interview. I actually did reasonably well at that, but there were no schools needing principals at that time, so I remained a deputy principal, despite the fact that for nearly three years, I had been the relieving principal of that school. After not attaining a principalship, I decided to retire from the public system.

Explanation

DET refers to the state government's Department of Education and Training.

Department: In the days when I was a teacher, faculties were usually called departments. So high schools had an English Department, a Maths Department, and so on. Today, schools tend to use "faculty" instead.

Inspectors: These were initially teachers who excelled and were promoted to a role where they would assess teachers for promotion. They usually belonged to a subject area. So the system had English inspectors, Science inspectors, and so on.

Lists: There were four lists:
List 1: This did not lead directly to any promotion in secondary schools. Passing this inspection meant that the teacher was quite competent and would probably go further. Before lists were abolished, an addendum to the list had the names of senior assistants on List 1. I was promoted to one of those.
List 2: This was the list for promotion to head of a department, a master or mistress. If your name was on the list, you could apply for promotion; appointments generally were made on seniority.
List 3: This was the list for promotion to deputy principal. The same rules as above applied to this list.
List 4: This was the list for promotion to principal. In my first years as a teacher, principals were known as headmaster or headmistress. Again, the same rules applied.

In those days, promotions were regulated by inspections. Inspectors would attend the school for a few days; they'd interview the applicant, sit in on their lessons, and decide if they were fit to pass the inspection.

Just before my last years as a teacher in the DET, promotions were by interview, something I was never very good at. A panel which included representatives of the DET was set up, and applicants were interviewed.

When I started teaching, without a degree, the only promotion I could aim at was to be a special secondary assistant in charge of a subject in a junior school. Teachers in high schools had to have a degree. Subject masters and mistresses in high schools had to have at least an honours bachelor's degree or a master's degree. In later times, it was found that not many teachers had the requirements. The regulations were changed so that a bachelor's degree plus an acceptable reading list would suffice. Principals were supposed to have a master's degree, but these rules eventually had to be abandoned, and the positions of principals came from the ranks of masters and mistresses of subjects. In 1969, a new classification came into being, that of form masters and mistresses. These were later called year patrons or year advisers. They received a special allowance in pay and often had their own office.

Chapter 2 may not be seen as being related to my teaching, but it really is. Having such a good friend and being accepted by a family helped me immensely. I felt comfortable with them, and they helped me to mature into a responsible adult. Young, single teachers taking up country appointments after having lived in the city usually find that joining in to the community will do wonders for their development.

1

Beginning

Working hours for teachers were ostensibly 9 a.m. to 3.30 p.m. (hours varied from school to school but had to be five hours and twenty minutes total teaching, (not including recess and lunch) but were really much longer than that for any teacher who was even a bit conscientious. I once worked out that I was sometimes spending more like eighty hours a week on schoolwork. I was usually half an hour early to school in the mornings and often stayed at least an hour late in the afternoon and usually took work home.

Typically, there were eight forty-minute periods each day: three periods before recess, then two before lunch, and then three more. This again varied from school to school. In later years, many school adopted fifty-minute periods, six in a day, often two before recess, two before lunch, and then two after lunch.

My first appointment was to Hurstville Secondary Junior Technical High School. It was for boys who didn't qualify to go to a proper high or intermediate high school. In other words, they were the leftovers. I refused to call them "dregs." As part of my Teachers College training, I had spent a practice session at the same school. This proved to be a handicap because every first-year teacher tries to hide the fact that they are just beginning, but these boys immediately knew that I was raw.

I met the head and his deputy and was given directions to find the staffroom. My desk was part of a huge table, loosely defined from others at the table. This staffroom was one of three in the school; the others were for the Manual Arts and Social Studies/English/History staff. The rest of our

1

staffroom had tables for the rest of the teachers who called the staffroom home. There was also table tennis, consisting of a big table with a suitably sized wooden board on top. We also had a darts board. Competitions were held for both recreational activities.

Al was one of the teachers who shared our table. He was notable in my eyes in that he spent every period when he was not teaching with his feet on the table and a copy of the daily newspaper in his hands. He was the most casual person I had ever met. He told me that the headmaster had visited his class one day. When the headmaster entered, he left the room. The headmaster explained that he wanted to talk to the class. Al replied, "One class, one teacher." At the end of the year, after all tests had been marked and reports prepared, one of the other teachers complained to the headmaster that Al had apparently not completed his reports. The headmaster confronted Al, who angrily replied that all was complete, and to prove it, he retrieved the work from his bag.

The headmaster had been a Maths teacher, and he would sometimes come into the classroom and show off his expertise as a teacher but whenever he came, he taught the same lesson, regardless of what the class was doing.

My teaching allocation was 1B Science; 1D Science; 1D Maths which in these days would be called 7B, 7D. In addition I had 2A, B, C, D, E, F, and G; and 3G Years 8 and 9) for Hobbies. I was also the roll teacher for 1D. In those days, class numbers were restricted to forty-eight. There were no textbooks either issued by the school or bought by the parents of the students. I had three maths textbooks, which I had bought on the advice of my lecturer in Teachers College, one each for Arithmetic, Algebra, and Geometry. This meant that in a Maths lesson, I had to copy all the exercises on the board. I taught Arithmetic, Algebra, and Geometry separately, so their workbooks had three sections.

On my first day of teaching, I recall asking a maths teacher how to start teaching algebra, and he told me to start with algebraic equations. In those days, "x" was the unknown, and we taught all the ways in which "x" would become the known. The textbooks I had bought helped me on our way. I don't recall the names of the Maths books, but I recall the authors of two of them. One was by Searle and Jones, and another was by Aitken and Farlow.

In later years, beginning teachers were given lots of help by the school administration, and courses were offered. Beginning teachers in the days when I started were very much on their own. If any help was given at all, it was done so grudgingly by teachers who felt that they were overworked anyway. One had to sink or swim.

In teaching Maths, I crafted lessons which included inductive and deductive discovery, as I had been taught at college. I sometimes wonder if the boys really took in the work I had carefully prepared. Mostly, the class did exercises I wrote on the board. In those days, problems in Arithmetic involved coping with the complexities of the imperial measurements of length and mass and the monetary system of pounds, shilling, and pence.

In later years of my teaching, I used to ask the students, by then thoroughly immersed in decimal systems, how they would cope with the following:

12 inches = 1 foot
3 feet = 1 yard
5½ yards = 1 rod, pole, or perch
4 rods, poles, or perches = 1 chain
22 yards = 1 chain
100 links = 1 chain
10 chains = 1 furlong
8 furlongs = 1 mile
Thus, one mile consisted of 5,280 feet or 1,760 yards.

Or
16 ounces = 1 pound
14 pounds = 1 stone
2 stones = 1 quarter
4 quarters = 1 hundredweight
20 hundredweights = 1 ton

Or
12 pence = 1 shilling
20 shillings = 1 pound

The extreme question students might be asked might be "How much would three quarters and five pounds of a substance cost at a price of two shillings and three pence per ounce?" Algebra, at least in first year, consisted of solving simple equations such as "3x + 5 = 26," while Geometry consisted of drawing circles with a pair of compasses, recognising shapes, and learning simple theorems.

I have seen a lot of Maths teachers in my time who, having set the work, sit at the front of the room and supervise the class. This was never part of my style. I moved around the room, looking at students' work, helping where it was seen that it was needed, correcting mistakes, ticking correct answers, adding comments such as "Well done," and so on. Students were always encouraged to ask for help or to comment. Gold and silver stick-on stars gave the students some reward.

From time to time, oral quizzes were given to find out if the students took in what was presented. Sometimes, written tests were given, again for diagnostic purposes.

At this school, I found that students tended to be fairly unresponsive. I had the feeling that many were there simply because they had to be, and fifteen years of age couldn't come quickly enough. Fifteen was the legal age at which students could leave school (except under special circumstances and only if they could start an apprenticeship).

As for Science, I had a couple of periods in a laboratory and the rest in the classroom. I must add that pupils stayed in the same room (their home room) for their all their lessons, except for their trips to the lab or to specialist rooms such as the woodworking room.

The Science I taught was really only combined Physics and Chemistry. There was no Biology, Geology, or Astronomy. In girls schools or coed schools, girls typically were taught Biology or Physiology and Hygiene. My wife recalled that when textbooks were handed out in her class, the section on the human reproductive system had been removed from the books.

I do not recall receiving any help in deciding what was to be my Science program. After consulting the syllabus for junior combined Physics and Chemistry classes, I just taught them Heat, Light, Sound, Magnetism, Electricity, and Mechanics. This seemed to work well and was, in those days, the standard course. I believe that the same curriculum had been in existence since before I was born. I discussed each topic with the class, spoke about lots of examples, performed appropriate experiments and demonstrations, and wrote notes on the board, and the boys copied the notes into their workbooks. Consequently, much of my time was spent at the front of the room; however, once I had developed confidence in my teaching, I moved about the room, supervising the students.

When we went to the laboratory once a week, I had to demonstrate every experiment. The boys were not allowed to touch any of the apparatus (in case they broke it). It also meant that I had a limited use of the blackboard (yes, it was black); the teacher who taught all the rest of the first-year (Year 7) classes had written his notes on half the board, and the notes stayed there for the whole week so that each of his classes had their notes already on the board, and he had to write them only once a week. That teacher had been teaching first-year Science for so long that no one could remember when he started, and he taught nothing else. Part of his teaching was that each boy had to copy his notes into their workbook. There was another Science laboratory in the school, but that was restricted to the use of second- and third-year classes (Years 8 and 9). It was hard to prepare material to demonstrate things to the class because the other teacher had control of all the equipment and frankly did not appreciate anyone else using his stuff. Consequently, Science was pretty boring.

I did my best to make it interesting, and when I demonstrated an experiment, I had the class move closer to the action. Some of the things I demonstrated I provided myself. Once I went to some stone masons near a cemetery, asking for slabs of marble when we were discussing calcium carbonate. I made several charts which I would show at the appropriate time. This laboratory was notable for the large number of pens adhering by their nibs to the ceiling. In those days, students wrote using pen and ink.

Braving all and thinking that it takes a fair bit to destroy a magnet, I issued magnets to the first-year class and invited them to play with them. I showed them a few tricks and invited the class to tell me what they discovered. You can learn a lot by playing with magnets, and they learned a lot. Yes, the magnets were carefully counted out and counted when returned, and yes, they were all returned.

Just sitting at their desks and rubbing their hands together vigorously for an extended period of time was an experiment which taught the students about friction as a source of heat. Pressing their ears to the bench or desktop while someone drummed their fingers on the wood showed the students that sound can travel through solid objects. There are a lot of experiments which can be performed without the use of scientific apparatus.

As the classes were working, answering questions, I moved around the room, checking, encouraging, commenting, although this was somewhat difficult because of the geography of the laboratory, students being seated at long benches with some ten students to each bench. One could only directly access students at each end of the long benches.

When I started with the hobbies classes, I asked each class what they wanted to do, and each class replied that they really wanted to get on with their own work. I began to see for myself why some teachers referred to social studies as "colouring in." True enough, several boys used their hobbies period to colour in their Social Studies workbook. They did their own work quietly, with no fuss.

One day, as I was supervising a hobbies class, a trio of boys came into the room. They had been given the job of painting the blackboards green. The decree had gone out that chalkboards would henceforth be green, with yellow chalk issued for writing on them. Chalkboards have been green ever since, except when they were supplanted by white boards and much later by smart boards. All went well with the painting, until the message boy came to the room with a request that the boy holding the paint tin was required by the headmaster. At this, the boy fainted and was covered in green paint. I was told some years later that he had completed his exams for the Intermediate Certificate (public exam at the end of third year) using green ink. The teachers wondered jokingly if I was responsible.

Message boys came from second year (Year 8). Each day, the next boy on the list had his turn until the roster began over again. They delivered messages from the headmaster to teachers during class time.

Students asking questions in class and making suggestions was not generally encouraged in teaching. Students had to absorb what was taught and be able to regurgitate it in the examinations held twice a year. In several cases, it was rote learning. It was the way teachers themselves had been taught at school, and who was going to challenge that? I did not agree with this method of teaching and actively encouraged questions and suggestions.

I was inspected once during this, my first year. On the advice of more experienced teachers, I had placed my better students in the four corners of the room, on the basis that inspectors often paused near the corners. I had also been advised to set up a situation where students knowing the correct answer to my questions would raise their right hand, while those who were not sure would raise their left hand. I thought about this but decided it could cause complications, so I didn't do it. However, I had told the students in one class where there were several unruly students what inspection meant for me. When the inspector was there, the miscreants behaved splendidly, answering all the questions. When the inspection was over, I thanked the class.

"That's okay," they said and promptly went back to their former ways.

The inspector was satisfied, and I passed that one.

One useful tip given to me by the inspector was that, in asking a question, name the student you want to answer the question after asking the query rather than before. His explanation was, "If you nominate the student before the question, the rest of the class need not trouble themselves."

With forty-eight unruly boys in class, each lesson was a battle to maintain discipline. The cane came in handy for reinforcing discipline. I think that every teacher in the school used the cane, carrying one with them to classes.

As a first-year teacher, I was not allowed to use the cane, but misbehaviour in classes became an issue, so after about three weeks, the members of the staffroom taught me how to cane boys. A stick of chalk was placed on a table, with part of it protruding over the side of the table. The trick was to clip the end of the chalk off without disturbing the rest of the stick.

Talking about chalk, another tip from experienced teachers was to get students to clean the board rather than doing it myself. The logic was that if you did it yourself all the time, you could get "dusted lungs," whereas if you asked a different student each time, they would be at negligible risk.

Boys were caned for misbehaviour, not doing homework, and other misdemeanours. From that time, I carried a cane into every classroom, and misbehaviour became manageable. At the time, using the cane did not cause me trouble. I had had the cane when I was a student in school.

One day, with no warning, the blackboard fell off the wall. As it landed, a shower of canes came also. That solved the mysterious disappearance of many canes. The class wags had been surreptitiously throwing canes over the top of the board, which had finally given way.

Playground duty was interesting and, as I discovered, dangerous. I attempted to break up a fight between two third-year boys who were going at each other with fists and boots. Another teacher saw me and thankfully drew me away in the interests of my safety. These two were eventually separated and taken away for the cane.

Punishments for all sorts of things in class were often to "pick up twenty papers at lunchtime and report to the teacher on duty." It was the task of the teacher on playground duty to check these when the culprit reported to him. The student carried a note from the teacher giving the punishment. This note, signed by the teacher on playground duty, was handed in next time the student was in the offended teacher's class. The crafty ones tore large papers into pieces and saved themselves much bending over. Teachers were rostered onto playground duty. They had to keep an eye on things, stop fights if necessary, and make sure that students kept the playground clean and tidy.

One day, while I was teaching a class, a siren sounded in the street outside the school. It was a fire truck. The entire class got up and ran to the windows to look out. I thought quickly; was this something I had to exert some discipline over? In the end, I did nothing, and the class soon returned to their desks. There are some things you will never control.

From time to time in class, we could hear the principal blowing into the microphone through the public-address system. There was one loudspeaker in each corridor. Each class had a public address monitor, who would jump up, open the door, and stand in the corridor to listen to the announcement. He would then repeat the message to the teacher. Nine times out of ten, it did not concern us.

One day, the announcement did concern us. Someone had stolen the brake blocks from a student's bike. He reported this to the headmaster, who then told the school that he knew who did it, and if the blocks were not on his desk by nine o'clock next morning, there would be hell to pay.

At the next staff meeting, the headmaster said that on the morning after this announcement, he could hardly see the wood on his desk for brake blocks and other parts of bikes. He reported on another nasty habit where jam tin lids had been operated on to produce two spikes: one to go into the ground, the other to protrude upwards after placing them on the school's driveway. The designer obviously had designs on tyres of teachers' cars.

I often visited the room where student record cards were kept and looked through them. As each student in public schools entered into kindergarten, a pupil record card was set up. This card was passed on as they went to higher schools. I remember one boy who had been described by his fifth-class teacher as "vindictive, vulpine and mendacious." I had to go get a dictionary. I couldn't match the description with the boy who, at that stage, was rather short for his age. I met this boy some twelve years later, working as a driveway assistant in a service station. He recognised me, and we had an enjoyable conversation. He was a likeable young man and was at least six feet tall (I didn't tell him what I had found on his card).

Teachers often smoked on playground duty and, in fact, as they signed in at the beginning of the day and at staff meetings. They didn't smoke in the classrooms. I joined in to the practice.

Teachers had to sign their name and what time they arrived at the school each day. The deputy (given the name "Sluggo" after a cartoon character at the time) complained at a staff meeting that it was impossible to have all the teachers arriving at 8.45, even those who came late. Teachers then began signing in at 8.44.01, then 8.44.02, and so on. He decided that he would put a red line under the signatures at 8.45 so he could catch the latecomers.

The next day, we saw a red line under every signature. Some wag on the staff had decided to torpedo that idea. Sluggo tried again. He obtained a number of metal disks, each with a number on it. These were hung on hooks on one side of a wooden board, and as teachers signed in, they were to transfer their disk to the other side of the board, indicating that they had signed in. I can still recall that my number was twenty-one. If a teacher forgot to transfer his disk, two boys were designated to carry the board to the room where the teacher was later in the day and request that he attend to the disk. This lasted a week, and then some of the disks went missing. Then more disappeared, and we knew that the wag had struck again. In the end, Sluggo gave up.

I have taught in schools where each teacher was allocated a number on the sign-on book and had to sign on opposite his number. (I refer to teachers as "him" all the time; there were no women on the staff, not even a secretary. There were no secretaries or ancillary staff then.

The Manual Arts staff had an ingenious method to save their teaching time. Manual arts classes were restricted to twenty-four. They combined two classes (there was room for that), with one teacher teaching the class while a second teacher sat at the back of the room to maintain discipline. I heard several years later that a Technical Drawing teacher, when rostered to be the disciplinarian, used to sit on a stool on top of a bench, overlooking everyone. The student who told me said that the teacher had drifted off to sleep one day and looked to be about to fall off the stool. The student told me that he had given the teacher a short sharp rap with a T-square to wake him up and had received the cane in response.

"But," he said, "I couldn't let the old bugger break his neck in a fall."

The Music teacher had a table near the door of our staffroom. At recess or lunchtime, there would sometimes be a knock at the door from a student who wanted to see a teacher. Spike Jones (the nickname we gave the teacher) would throw the door open, drag the poor unfortunate in by the scruff of the neck, and berate the pupil for disturbing his lunch before asking what he wanted. Only the brave considered knocking on our door.

Sometimes, there would be a few teachers who had a period off in the staffroom. Teachers in those days taught twenty-eight forty-minutes periods in a week. Each day consisted of eight periods, except for sports days, when the day consisted of five periods, with the afternoon three periods long. Teachers had nine periods a week off. This time was supposed to be used to prepare lessons, mark work, or other things. Teachers who were off often struck up a game of table tennis in our staffroom. This was until the headmaster burst in one day and roundly told off the players for not preparing lessons and marking books.

The teachers in the staffroom got on well, and several would retire to the pub after school and wash their problems away. Friday afternoons were a favourite time for this. I rarely took part, as I had quite a distance to drive home. My last contact with the teachers occurred on the last day of the school year, when nearly all the staff went to the pub.

During the May vacation, I bought a second-hand car. Our family had moved, and we lived some distance from the school, entailing long journeys in the train.

The car was a 1934 Vauxhall 14/6 (14 horsepower/six cylinders). The car was a small, high-sided sedan with an all-metal body, although the centre portion of the roof was made separately. I think that when cars of this vintage were made, they did not have the technology to make the entire body shell in one piece. The car was a four-seater, with bench seats front and back. Both the gear stick (four forward and reverse) and the handbrake sat in the middle of the front floor. There were four pedals because as well as the accelerator, foot brake, and clutch, this car also had a foot starter. The idea was, you turned on the ignition, engaged neutral, pulled out the choke, and pushed the foot starter until the engine fired up. If the engine stalled, you couldn't start it with the clutch depressed because you used your left foot on the starter. The car also had a hand throttle, which you could pull out on a long journey, acting like a cruise control (provided that the road was flat). The brakes were mechanical, requiring a massive effort to stop. The foot brake operated on all four wheels, but the hand brake operated only on the rear wheels. You had to grease the system every five hundred miles; otherwise, the brakes would stay on once applied, and you had to put your foot under the pedal to pull them back off.

I took driving lessons. The last one was the driving test, which was held on the first day of the second term. I passed the test and drove to school, arriving late. As I parked the car, I encountered the headmaster, who enquired if I had been sick. I innocently told him the reason I was late (under the circumstances which then transpired, I should have said that I had been sick). He admonished me to not do it again, to which I replied, "No. I have my licence now." Oh, the innocence of the young.

In March, I had to go into camp with the Sydney University Regiment. This was my last year of my national service. We went to Singleton. While we were in camp, it rained all week, and Singleton became flooded. The regiment had gone into the bush for field exercises. I stayed in camp with a few others because I had developed the flu. After several days, they brought the regiment back in. They were like drowned rats. All military stuff was abandoned, and the regiment set about cleaning up the town of Singleton. One of the jobs I was involved in was shovelling mud out of the Catholic church.

During the time I spent at this school, moves were being made for women teachers to receive equal pay. In those days, they did not, but at the same time, prices for women to attend various types of entertainment such as movies or the horse races were lower than they were for men. Equal pay eventually came in.

On the day of the athletics carnival, the entire school marched to the local sports oval. All the competitions went well. I was assigned supervision of spectators. At lunchtime, a few of the staff went to the local hotel. This did not go well with the headmaster, who suspended them for the rest of the day. I thought that this must be a way to get a half a day off. No other action was taken on the miscreants.

One period a week was allocated to scripture classes. I was assigned Anglican scripture in a large covered assembly area, where a minister taught all the Anglicans in one large group. There were several teachers allocated to this group. Their job was to maintain discipline.

"Put that cigarette out, mister." This was how I was addressed at a staff meeting during my first year. It was quite offensive because the headmaster used "mister" when addressing the students at the school. Older members of staff told me that he liked to bully the first-year teachers but wasn't game to attack the older staff.

Staff meetings were held from time to time in the entrance hall. It was customary for teacher to smoke if they wished. I was a smoker and lit up, only to get that admonishment referred to earlier. Others in the meeting put their smokes out with me. This was the straw that broke the camel's back. My request for a transfer was on the principal's desk next morning.

It was not until the early eighties that restrictions were put on smoking in schools. It was initially confined to smoking only in common rooms and staffrooms, but later, smoking was prohibited in any part of school grounds, forcing some members of staff to have to stand outside the school for their smoko.

At the end of the year, I was invited to set the annual examination for the first-year Science students. I thought I would set an exam using true/false and multiple choice questions. This I did. After the children did the examination, the teachers who had supervised the exam complained that the boys had finished the one-hour exam in thirty minutes and were then a nuisance to control. It took a long time before I used multiple choice again, and I never resorted to true/false questions after that.

I don't recall a lot of the things which went on in the classroom, but this one incident sticks in my mind. Various items of students' possessions went missing, most likely stolen. Near the end of the school day, one student complained that his pen had been stolen. I had had just about enough of this and announced that when the bell rang for the end of the day, we would stay in class until someone owned up as having stolen the pen. The whole class, including the victim, were to stay in.

Five minutes went by, then ten, when the victim put his hand up and said, "Sir, I have just found my pen. I had dropped it on the floor."

I said, "I'll give you a one-minute head start before the rest of the class can go home. Do you have anything to say to the class?"

Curiously, when it came to Higher School Certificate (HSC) exams in the sixties, the Level 2F and 2S Science exams were completely multiple choice. The initial 2F exam contained 270 questions, of which candidates had to answer 180 questions. This was because the syllabus had been shortened to two-thirds of its original size, but the choice of which third of the original syllabus was not taught was left to schools. The poor students not only had to answer the questions but decide which questions they would answer. This disaster never occurred again.

At the end of the year, it was customary for students to give the teacher a card or a present. I received only one present: a bottle of Mudgee Mud, a beer concocted by a brewery in Mudgee. Shortly after this, the brewery shut down (the beer was horrible).

When I became a teacher on a government scholarship, we all had to agree to spend at least two years in country service. Apart from the fact that I wanted to get away from the headmaster, I also wanted to remake myself. I was thoroughly dissatisfied with who I was and wanted to recreate myself and do my country service. I applied to be sent to, in order, North Coast region, South Coast region, and Southern Highlands. I got Far West. The Far West was given an extra week of Christmas holidays because of the hot climate experienced. When I got my appointment, I had to look it up on the map.

Altogether, my first year was a baptism of fire. Teaching these children was really hard. To start with, they were the remainders of the education system. They had failed to go to academic schools, and many of them were bad behaviour cases. Some teachers were by and large quite content to teach in that school for the rest of their lives, having no desire to do anything else.

Okay, I must admit that attitude might apply to many, many people, but it simply was not good enough for me. My main reason for wanting to go to the country was the opportunity to start again and not fall into the pitfalls I had experienced in my first year. Despite all the problems I had at this school, I wanted to go on teaching. My love of children was to come later.

During this year, I decided to enrol at one of the universities. I received some credit for subjects I had passed in another university before I went to Teachers College. I began university study at the University of Technology (later called the University of NSW) but gave it up halfway through the year. I passed one subject, Engineering Materials. However, trying to do this and teach became too much, and I quit university studies. When I moved to the country, I tried again and later managed to complete a bachelor's degree.

Because this will come up later, I must mention that I broke off with my girlfriend (who later became my wife). We were not to meet again for ten years.

2

Leaving Home

A letter in the mail. Official. Department of Education. My application for a posting to North Coast, South Coast, or Southern Tablelands? Which one did I get? Dad! Where is Cobar? Oh! Far West? Oh well, we will see.

A visit to the local parish priest to tell him that I will soon no longer be a parishioner and, by the way, what do you know about Cobar. He knew a lady in the parish who had connections.

I visited her with lots of questions. One of them was, "Do they have electricity there?" She assured me that they did, but it was from a local generator which switched off at midnight every night to come back at six o'clock the next morning. She gave me the name of a lady I might look up when I got to my new appointment.

I started to pack. I thought that I would visit my previous school on their first day to say farewell. Because my new appointment was in the Far West of the state, I had an extra week of school holidays because that part of the state gets very hot in the summer months which, as I must remind my Northern Hemisphere friends, is in December, January, and February.

The DET had kindly suggested that the accommodation I might consider was a hotel. Some teachers had stayed there. I contacted the hotel in question and booked in.

I loaded my 1934 Vauxhall with my teaching aids and all the clothes I possessed. A few days before school began, off I went, leaving my mother crying at the kerbside. I guess that she was recalling the time when she left home to work. I decided that I would drive to the west via Bells Line of Road, a pretty drive over the Blue Mountains Range to the west of Sydney but with some steep hills. Going up was a slow, laborious task for the old car, but going down was somewhat terrifying because mechanical brakes are not noted for quick slowdowns. I vividly recall rounding the last bend coming into Lithgow. It was, to say the least, touch and go. I made it and determined that I would not take that route again, at least not in that direction.

The distance to my new destination was quite large, so I had booked into a hotel in Dubbo, halfway to my destination for the first night. The next day, I was off again and into the rain, which had commenced during the night. Once I got out into the west, I ran into a single-lane road, one car wide. The idea was that oncoming traffic moved to one side, and you did also. You usually had one wheel on the bitumen and the other in the dirt. The first time I had to do this, I dutifully moved over until the other car had passed and then made the huge mistake of accelerating while one wheel was on the bitumen and the other was in the mud. The car swerved violently, tipping with two wheels in the air. I recall seeing the road through the passenger's side window before things settled. The car had stopped at right angles to the road, with my foot firmly pressed on the brake, clutch not touched, and the engine stopped.

Gingerly, I turned the car around and resumed the journey, having learned an important lesson: Don't accelerate with one wheel in the mud. The farther I went, the worse the roads became until there was no more bitumen, and I began to learn how to drive with all wheels on mud. By the way, that rain continued, and shortly after I got to my destination, the place was flood-bound, with supplies having to be air-dropped to us.

I eventually arrived at my destination and found the hotel. It was an old hotel with a back yard where I could park the car. Each room had two occupants. A mosquito net was provided, thankfully, because the mosquitoes were bad. Later that first day, other new teachers arrived, having travelled to the town by train. We met and did what many Australians do on such occasions: we went downstairs to the bar and had a beer.

It was at the bar in this hotel that I learned another life-saving lesson. I had got myself involved with a group of locals who were indulging in another Australian tradition: "shouting." To the uninitiated, shouting means that each person takes it in turn to buy drinks for the whole group. This is common among Australian men. I got to the stage when I felt that I had had enough. So I turned my glass upside down on the counter.

Immediately, an arm came over my shoulder, and the hand attached to it turned my glass up the right way, and a voice said, "Do you really want to fight everyone in the bar?"

Apparently, turning one's glass over was an invitation to a fight.

"Just put your hand over the glass when the barmaid comes to refill the glasses," he said.

My new place was quite hot, and I spent more than a little time in the hotel bar. One day, a local asked if I wanted to have a game of darts. "First to reach 57." My turn first. I had had a little practice at my previous school, so I aimed and hit the wire separating 19 from triple 19. The dart slipped into the single 19. Had it gone the other way, I would have had 57 in one go. From there on my darts went the usual way: all over the board and sometimes missing the board altogether. My opponent on the day nearly had a heart attack.

I soon discovered that I had not packed any shoe polish, so I went to the shopping centre, looking for a likely shop. When I found the shop, it was right next to another hotel. My journey to the shop in question was interrupted by, firstly, a paddy wagon (a police truck with a cage on the back) screeching to a stop outside the hotel and police running into the hotel. Then, a patron of the hotel came hurtling through the door horizontally, having been pitched there by the local constabulary, who picked him up, shoved him into the cage, and drove off. I managed to get the shoe polish.

After turning a tap on to have a glass of water in my hotel, I found out that water was not for drinking; only water collected on the roof and channelled into a water tank was potable. The tap water was so hard that you needed lots of water softener to do the clothes washing.

I did look up the lady who had been referred to me, and she said that she would introduce me to some of the local boys my age. This she did, having dinner at her house, and I was introduced to Clive and Leon. I hit it off immediately with Clive, and we became firm friends. Clive had a motorbike and sidecar, an old Indian with a gear stick on the right-hand side. Clive was a motor mechanic and the projectionist at the local cinema. He had a twin sister, and I was invited to join the family each Sunday night to play cards: 500.

I had never played 500, so I had to learn quickly. We played six-handed 500, and before long, I had learned the correct cards to play. Woe betide you if you played the "wrong card". It was often said that we were "playing for a sheep station." In other words, it was taken seriously. Still, the family were very friendly and supportive. Clive was a singer. His brother said that he could have made a career as a singer, and that was true. He had a magnificent tenor voice. His mother played the piano. In her younger days, she had played the piano during silent movies before sound movies came. We had many great sing-songs at their place.

Clive's family also had a dog and a cat. During the winter, as the family sat around the fire, the cat and dog lay there in front of the fire, often with the cat resting her head on the dog. The dog sometimes tried to rest his head on the cat, reversing the scene, but the cat would have none of that. One night, a stray cat ambled casually into the room (no one locked their doors). There was an immediate reaction by the dog and cat, and then, no stray cat. Pause five seconds, and then the cat fell out of the chimney, somewhat singed and blackened from trying to climb up and out. One second later, no stray cat, as it hightailed out of the room, never to be seen again.

I seemed to fall easily to living in the country. The town was miles from anywhere else, and we had to make our own fun. Playing cards with the Commonwealth Bank staff was one way. The Commonwealth Bank had set up living quarters for their staff. They provided the rooms and the facilities. It was up to the staff to cook for themselves and keep the place clean. They had a spacious living room and invited the teachers to join them in card games. One night, we played poker for matches. The sort of matches I mean are those used to light a fire. We bought the matches at one penny each before the game. I remember winning one night, but when I went to cash in the matches, there were not enough pennies to cover the matches I had won. We didn't play there after that night.

At that stage, the town had no swimming pool. Clive and I and a few other friends would sometimes visit one of the dams (scrapes in the ground where pools of water would settle). We'd go in for a swim and then lay on the bank and cool off. The problem was that we had to get rid of the leeches we collected as we swam in the dam.

Another way I used to cool off was to hose myself down and sit on the veranda, reading a book until the wetness evaporated. While I was in the country, I began my university studies again, using distance education. I joined the tennis club and the golf club, and while tennis was no stranger to me, golf was; I had to get a set of golf clubs and then learn to use them. The golf course was hard-baked clay on the fairways, with very little grass, and the greens were of oiled sand. You could play a good shot, only to have it hit a pebble and ricochet off into the rough. The sand greens were tricky to play, and one was expected to one-putt the green once you were on it. After school started, I joined the staff competition, where one could challenge another member of staff to play on a specially selected nine holes. The winner would replace the loser on the competition ladder.

The town cinema had a dual seating plan. If it wasn't raining or too cold, the seating was in the open air. A series of parallel steel pipes supported deck chairs, which were quite comfortable. If the movie became boring, we could look at the stars. I became interested in the stars because I saw so many meteors crossing the sky, but that is another story. In case of rain or chilly weather, the film projectors were turned around to point the other way, and we sat in a normal cinema. Sometimes, we would start in the open air, only to have it rain halfway through the evening's entertainment and move inside. The seats inside were not bolted to the floor because the cinema was sometimes used for other purposes. One night, as we moved into the theatre, a patron bumped into one of the back seats, which sent all the chairs to tip over, one after another, like dominoes.

There were always two movies each session, so we had an interval between the shows. Our favourite drink was a spider, flavoured crushed ice. Once school started, a bunch of the teachers used to attend the movies, sitting in the back row. We used to comment, probably too loudly, on things which came up in the movie. While watching *Doctor in the House* with them one night, we came across that scene where the young doctor placed the stethoscope on the chest of a rather buxom young lady and asked for "big breaths," to which she replied, "Yeth, and I'm only thixteen." We howled so much that the rest of the patrons who hadn't understood the incident were shushing us.

At the end of my first year, I had saved enough money to buy a new car, a Morris Minor. It was a small car but more than enough for what I wanted. It had been driven up from Sydney but arrived with a broken gear box. I had to delay my trip home for the end-of-year school holidays for it to be fixed. It was a great car; I had it for five years before trading it in.

Driving in the country at night was somewhat hazardous due to kangaroos. They would appear out of nowhere at the side of the road and attempt to cross the road right in front of the car. Hitting one not only did great damage to the kangaroo (often killing it), it also did a lot of damage to the car. One of my friends hit one and dented the radiator of the car so much that he was unable to continue. I hit one coming home from visiting friends on a sheep station, thankfully at only ten miles per hour (I had caught up with a huge mob of them at night and was carefully trying to slip through). The kangaroo met its fate, but the car was unscathed. If we had to travel at night outside the town, all passengers had to stay alert and shout, "Roo," if they saw one. The driver would immediately apply the brakes and say, "Where?"

In my second year in this school, a new headmaster was appointed. The staff decided to drive to the next town, Nyngan where there was a swimming pool. Off we went in our cars. The new headmaster had a new car, and soon, we were eating his dust. Just before the new town, the road took a sharp 90 degree turn across the railway line. By the time I arrived at that spot, we were greeted with the sight of the headmaster's car on its side. The headmaster was being attended by the town ambulance officers. The poor man had broken his leg. He ended up in plaster for several months and had to rely on a walking stick for the rest of his life.

As I was driving to the school to start my second year, I came to a train crossing. I thought that this was about the time when the train would be approaching this crossing. I looked right and left, saw nothing, and crossed. I hadn't moved more than a hundred metres from the crossing when the train hove into view. I had missed it by less than fifteen seconds. When I had first looked, the train was hidden by trees.

The town loved to have dances and balls. I had inherited a dinner suit from a friend's father and got some use out of it. Clive and his sister and some staff attended the dances and balls, and we had a wonderful time with old-time dancing. I had been a drummer in the school band and borrowed a drum kit on some occasions to play for the dances. Clive, of course, did the singing.

Other amusements included occasional trips to Nyngan and Bourke, regardless of distance, for a swim in their pool and visits to sheep stations (the graziers were very friendly), and on one momentous occasion, we travelled 458.4 km to Broken Hill to watch a football match.

After the town recovered from being flood-bound, it didn't rain for about three years. During that time, a big dam (scrape in the ground) was built, with not one day being lost because of the weather.

During this time, a new policeman was appointed to the town. Doing his rounds one night, he was accosted by one of the locals and was soundly beaten up for no reason, just hooligan behaviour. After recovering, the policeman allegedly said, "You can beat me but you can't beat these buttons" (referring to the metal buttons bearing the police logo). Sure enough, two nights later, the police sergeant plucked the hooligan out of the hotel bar, and that was the last time that poor unfortunate ever picked on a member of the cops.

I like organising things and once organised a car meeting. We had races and trials on the local aerodrome (no planes that day). It went well, but there weren't many cars. I am afraid that the Morris Minor wasn't much good at the standing quarter-mile.

The person who owned the cinema also owned the billiard saloon and was also the local starting price bookmaker.

After several months of boarding at the hotel, some of us decided to look for another place. We found one with an old lady who provided meals, including a cut lunch. She also did the clothes washing. The accommodation was very crowded, with three beds in one room, where two would have filled the space. Dinner each night consisted of cold boiled mutton. Sandwiches were the same. We negotiated with the lady to stop providing lunch and chose to get our own. We tolerated the conditions to the end of the first year and then decided to rent a house.

Five of us moved in. We set up a roster system for cooking, cleaning, and washing. The system went very well. None of us knew much about cooking, so we invited the women on the staff to come to dinner at night and show us how to cook. After we became proficient, we invited them to come to dinner as our guests. As I say, all went well, until one of our number decided to marry one of the local girls. They had to have a separate bedroom, of course, and things became somewhat awkward. I moved to private boarding in my last year, and this proved to be better.

The lady in this place was a very conservative Christian. She didn't approve of playing cards, and Sunday nights were devoted to listening to hymns broadcast from the local radio. The tunes were very recognisable to me. I had heard them before with different words sung as ditties in the army. The ditties in the army would not have passed the censor. I really couldn't listen to those hymns without the salacious words going through my brain. Fortunately, Sunday night was card night at Clive's house, so I was safe. The husband of this landlady had retired several years ago having worked in the mines and getting "dusted lung. He spent much of the week looking up the form of the racehorses, ready to place his ten shillings (one dollar) bet on Saturday. Two women teachers also boarded here.

One of the women boarders was the Home Science teacher. She remarked one day that the industrial arts teacher had asked her to accompany him to a dance. I began to laugh which, of course, brought the young lady to tears; she demanded that I explain. I apologised for the hurt I had caused and explained that the Industrial Arts teacher had tried valiantly to interest the previous Home Science teacher, who had rejected all his approaches. As it turned out, the two later married and lived happily ever after.

What of school? Next chapter, please.

3

Country Teaching

The new staff and I (five of us) duly turned up on the first day to meet the headmaster and deputy headmaster and infants mistress of Cobar Intermediate High. They all seemed friendly enough; we were given our timetables and told where to sit in the staffroom and began our first day of teaching. Not being a university graduate at that stage, I had only junior classes for Mathematics and Science, together with one class of English. Classes were small, and for the first time, I had to cope with girls.

The best thing for me was that I had a desk. Desks had been built in the staffroom in a line, fastened to the wall. Not only did I have a space to myself, the desk had a bookshelf above it and a cabinet in which I could store my teaching materials.

I found out that the teacher I was replacing was known to me. He apparently did not have a successful time at the school, and students made a lot of fun of him. Many years later, when I was a deputy principal, responsible for hiring substitute teachers, I received a note from the head office instructing all schools not to hire the same teacher. I have no idea what the teacher had done since I heard of him last, but it must have not met with the approval of the DET.

It took me only five minutes in class to learn another important lesson. One girl asked me if she could leave the room to get a glass of water. I told her to wait until recess. As the lesson progressed, her face became redder and redder, and she began to cry. I asked her what was the matter. She tearfully replied that she needed to go to the toilet. Well, of course, I said she could go. Since that day, I never refused any girl who wanted to leave the room, regardless of what she said she wanted to do. Boys still had to wait until recess.

Being a twenty-two-year-old male, as a lot of young men do, I became attractive to Year 7 students, twelve-year-old girls who, when they came to me at the front of the room, tended to try to snuggle up to me, standing toe to toe. I had a wooden ruler on my desk. I'd apply gentle pressure on their abdomen with the ruler, pushing them away to a respectable distance. They got the message. I have always been very wary of any contact with girls in my care. These days, I could end up being sued or in trouble with the law if I were to touch a girl. I might give a boy a tap on the shoulder if I thought he needed to give more attention to his work.

Later, during that first week, I was walking down a corridor leading to the staffroom. Ahead of me was an open door with a screen door obscuring the view of the room. There was something going on there. I couldn't work out what it was, but as I approached, I watched intently. The door suddenly slammed, to my astonishment, and I wondered what was going on. A quick enquiry established that the door led to the girls change room in the Home Science department. It was obvious what had happened. A quick word to the Home Science teacher about closing the door fixed that one.

I was introduced to the school's Science laboratory (yes, the only one). It shared a building with the Industrial Arts room, either end of the same building. No gas had been connected to the lab, so I wondered what we did for heating test tubes. I soon found out: we used spirit burners. Each burner had a small tank of methylated spirits. There was also a cup surrounding the barrel of the burner. One poured a little methylated spirit into this cup and set it alight. This drew the metho up, and before long, one had a Bunsen flame.

The only trouble was that the whole thing was liable to catch fire, as I learned during my first practical lesson. It happened at one bench, and the kids at that bench, being used to this sort of thing, quickly pushed their books to one side and turned off the methylated spirit. Within seconds, the whole thing was over, and we got back to business. I determined that first-year (Year 7) kids were going to do experiments, actually touch apparatus, not like my previous school, where they were forbidden to touch any apparatus in case they broke it.

The school had very little Science equipment, but we (there was one other faculty member teaching Science and Mathematics) made do with what we had. In consequence, much of the course I taught was theoretical.

At this stage, I had acquired quite a library of Science magazines. These were made available to students of all classes.

Not having an English teaching background, I struggled with teaching it. Fortunately, the headmaster and another teacher helped, and I didn't do too badly. In later years, I was assigned to an art class (I'll discuss that later).

As it transpired, one of the students at the school had died during the Christmas vacation. This was felt greatly by the students, as he was well liked. The school had acquired some textbooks, mostly novels, for study. When it came to reissue some textbooks, several students declined receiving any book that bore his name.

We found out that the school, like probably every house in town, was not locked until the end of term, so we virtually lived in the staffroom. This was far better than trying to live in the hotel where we stayed. I had my toothbrush, shaving equipment, and so on at school, close at hand.

Our headmaster (who later went on to bigger and higher things in the DET) was a stickler for getting things right. We had to have all our programs written out by the end of the first two weeks of term. This meant that we had to plan all our lessons in advance: a big job for teachers just starting (or, in my case, with one year's experience). We got to the task, spending many hours in the staffroom at night until we were ready to present our efforts to the headmaster.

Later, in the middle of the year, when temperatures were close to freezing, we spent virtually half the night in the staffroom, writing up our programs. We had a roaring fire going to keep us warm. Promptly at midnight, off went the lights, as the town generator turned off. We had to call it off. I volunteered to drive everyone home, but it was so cold that I couldn't get the car to start, so everyone had to grope their way home in the dark.

During my first term at the school, the headmaster began inspecting workbooks from all the classes. He collected the students' Arithmetic work books from my first-year class. I was subsequently called to his office to be told that I had not done enough work with the class; the sixth-class books had more work in them. I asked him if he had looked at the other Maths books from that class. The students, as you may recall, had three workbooks: Arithmetic, Algebra, and Geometry. He had collected only the Arithmetic books. When we compared our workbooks with those of sixth class, we had done at least twice as much as they. I also had the temerity to say that I didn't think that volume translated into quality teaching.

The headmaster also had a fetish about margins in workbooks. Students had to draw a margin the width of a ruler down the left-hand side of each page. The headmaster wanted students to rule the same coloured margin on each page. He was not concerned about what colour, red, black, green even, so long as the same colour was used on each page. He deplored "harlequin" margins. Another teacher and I spent some half an hour or more after one of our staff meetings arguing with him, our premise being that we were lucky if the kids ruled a margin at all, let alone what colour it was.

After this meeting, I went to the stationery shop and bought one of those pencils with three different coloured leads in it. You could use whatever colour you wanted by turning the pencil over to the desired colour. The next time I presented my programs to the principal, I ruled my margins with that pencil, rolling the pencil as I went so that each margin changed colour over and over from top to bottom: a true harlequin margin. No more from the headmaster on that subject.

The secondary staff had only one woman (Home Science) on it. She was very good at tennis. When it came to sports day (Wednesday afternoons), she took kids for tennis. Another man and I took the girls who didn't do tennis for sport. For girls, that consisted of playing a game called vigoro in the summer months and basketball in the cooler months. Women's basketball has changed a lot and is now called netball. Vigoro was based on cricket but had its own bats, balls, and rules.

The boys' sports were cricket in the summer and football (rugby league) in the cooler months. Some played tennis. The ground where the boys played football was a claypan as hard as a rock. One sports afternoon while umpiring the girls at sport, we heard a sharp and loud crack. We wondered what it was. It was, in fact, the femur bone of one of the boys playing football. Umpiring women's basketball was new to me so, I had to learn from the headmaster's wife; I even sat for an umpire's exam.

The school was in a three-school district competition. Each year, Cobar would play Bourke on Bourke's grounds, Bourke would play Nyngan on Nyngan's grounds, and Nyngan would play Cobar on Cobar's grounds. The following year, the process would be reversed. The school that won two out of three competitions won the trophy for the year. I was lucky to be picked to accompany our kids to Bourke one year. At this stage, we had already won against Nyngan. We needed to win this visit to win the trophy. The competitions were tennis, women's basketball, football, athletics, and debating. The last sport was football.

During the women's basketball competition, an argument came up between the wife of the headmaster, who was our umpire, and the umpire of the other school. It was about how the umpiring would be organised. The wife lost the argument, and as the first game proceeded, she made comments about the umpiring of the other umpire. She had a group of girls surrounding her. I managed to entice the group over to the other side of the court where I was. I made it clear that commenting about the officials, as she was, was unacceptable.

When we got to the last game, the scores were even. We had won tennis and women's basketball and debating. Winning the trophy for the year hung on the result of the football game. If we won that, we won against that school and the whole competition for that year.

Nearing the end of the football game, we were one point down. We had scored a try just before the bell rang, indicating the end of the game. The kick was to be taken on the sideline by Ernie, our star kicker, who had missed two previous attempts to kick a goal in the game. Everyone stood there transfixed, chewing fingernails. Ernie lined the ball up carefully and walked back. He ran forward and kicked. The ball sailed through the air and cleared the crossbar between the posts: goal and two points. We won. I was immediately swamped by a group of girls who had been standing nearby. They were over the moon.

The town had an aboriginal problem, or should I say, the problem was not with the aborigines but with the whites. At that time, aboriginals in Australia were not counted as being citizens, and in fact, they were considered to be part of the native fauna of the country and were badly treated by the white people. Since the competition was held over two days, we had decided to go to the cinema one night. Whites went upstairs, while aboriginals had to go downstairs (apartheid in action).

Our school produced an annual magazine. I decided that I would volunteer to become the school photographer. This was okay with the headmaster, and I went ahead. I took sporting photos and class photos, and they appeared in the magazine each year. I also supplied the local newspaper with photos. I went into the business of developing and printing my own photos at the school (they were, of course, black and white). I made my own light box for this task. My darkroom was one of the classrooms at night, with only the dim light from outside penetrating to help me see what I was doing.

My interest in Astronomy grew while I was at this school, as I used to marvel at the number of meteors I could see during boring bits at the open-air cinema. I decided that I would set up an Astronomy club at the school. I duly applied for an Astronomy kit from an organisation which loaned these kits to groups of people who were interested. The club went well with the kids, and many of them developed a lifelong interest in astronomy. I read as many of the books that came with the kit as I could. I noticed a discrepancy in one piece of data and contacted Sydney Observatory for clarification. The government astronomer explained that recent discoveries had updated the data, and he then asked if I would like to join the British Astronomical Association (New South Wales Branch). This I ultimately did and was introduced to variable star observing, which I did for several years.

While we had the kit, I developed a bad case of influenza and spent a week in bed. During that time, I read a book called *And There Was Light*. This history of astronomy had a profound influence on my life.

In 1957, the world was astounded when the Soviet Union put up Sputnik, the first artificial satellite. The Americans were taken totally off guard. They desperately worked to finish the rocket they were planning to use to send a satellite into space, and within weeks, they sent their effort skywards, only to have it fail. They immediately earned the title of "Pfutnik" (they did eventually get a satellite into orbit). I recall standing in the schoolyard one night watching as Sputnik went overhead. It was awesome.

One year, my allocation included Art for one class. I applied for an Art kit from the place where I had borrowed the Astronomy kit. I am no artist, but the kit taught me a lot about art. I could draw a face that looked like almost human. I learned all about perspective and other things. I even held an art competition in one of my Mathematics classes. The kids had to make up a painting using mathematical instruments: rulers, compasses, and so on. Colour was encouraged. The principal was invited to judge the competition.

Each Monday, a school assembly was held. The students proclaimed their allegiance to Australia, to the Queen, and to God. The usual notices were read, and awards were given out. The Australian flag figured importantly in this assembly.

In the middle of each year, an athletics carnival was held. This included the usual running races (100, 220, and 440 yards, and a mile), relay races, hurdles, long jump, high jump, shot put, discus, and so on. On the way to the grounds where the competitions were held, the kids paraded through the main street of the town. One year, when it was particularly cold and while the staff were well rugged up against the cold, the kids just wore their athletics uniforms. This did not go well with residents in the town.

Regular dances were held in the school. Several of the classrooms in the school had demountable walls; a space was cleared, and some local musicians were hired for the night. I became the teacher in charge of socials, as the dances were called. The kids loved them. Another regular event was the annual concert. Not only did the classes put on a play or an act, the staff did also. This was held in the open air at the school.

As previously mentioned, textbooks were rare; we relied on being able to print some of our material. The staff had access to a Fordigraph machine, which was a spirit duplicator. We made out a master copy (using colour, if available). This master copy could produce about fifty copies before the master ran out, if we were lucky. The headmaster had a Gestetner for his use. This used inks and a wax sheet. It could produce many copies. Before we could print anything, we had to ask permission. Money was scarce.

Many of the students at the school lived in the country, often so far away that they had to be accommodated in the town. The locals had built a hostel near the school to house these kids. One teacher had free housing and had to look after the kids while not at school. The hostel was also the town's war memorial. Each Anzac Day march made its way to the hostel.

Country towns had their local shows, where local produce was put on display. There would be judging of livestock, sideshow stalls, and so on. As part of the school's display, I recruited and trained a girls marching squad. We found an old side drum in the school store. This was restored, and I taught one of the girls how to drum. The leader had to be taught how to give orders, and the girls had to be taught the drills. This was much appreciated by the townsfolk. My mother even made a special epaulette for the leader to wear.

One day, I had asked the class to learn the statement and proof of a mathematical theorem. One student, a girl, volunteered to recite the work she had learned overnight. The words came out slowly with much hesitation, and I found myself grimacing as she stumbled over them. She took the grimaces as disapproval and began to cry, whereupon I heaped praise on her for being the only one who had done what I had asked. Another lesson for me.

I recalled an experiment my Physics teacher at school set up and repeated the experiment. It involved making a large coil of wire into which a steel rod was inserted. The coil was connected to a 240V AC power supply, and the steel rod was placed at one end of the coil, with one end of the rod just resting on the opening of the coil. All this was carefully prepared and set up before the class came into the room. I said nothing and proceeded with the lesson, ignoring the growing curiosity of the class regarding the coil and the rod. Eventually, the curiosity became questions from the students, and I asked if they wanted to know what the gadget was.

"Oh," I said, "I have been researching the idea of making an electromagnetic gun and thought that I would try something out." Fortunately, as it turned out, the coil was pointing along the teacher's bench and not at the class. "Do you want to see how it works?"

They did. I reached for the switch of the power point and gave it a quick on and off.

That rod shot into the coil like a rabbit into its burrow and came out the other side at high speed, smashing into the door, fortunately, otherwise goodness knows where it would have landed. When my teacher at school had performed that experiment, the rod went into the coil and stayed there. The class was most impressed and wanted more. It didn't take me long to say that the experiment needed some modifications and that I would leave it for the time being. After that lesson, I never repeated it on the consideration that it was far too dangerous. It did, however, give the class a greater understanding of the power of electromagnetism.

By the way, headmasters and headmistresses were renamed principals while I was a teacher at this school.

I stayed at this school for four years; I honed my skills, and when I eventually left, I was quite happy with my teaching. I was in love with teaching, and I was in love with children.

Having fewer students in classes was a boon. It meant that more time could be spent on individual students. Behaviour was not a problem. Several students came from sheep stations, where they had responsibilities. Many could drive a car or truck or motorbike, even though they were legally underage. By and large, they behaved admirably.

Students at this school reacted well to my teaching. They were not hesitant about asking questions and making comments. I encouraged them in this and praised those who participated.

I believe that I matured a lot at this school. I learned some very important lessons about teaching girls, not only about their requests to leave the room but how they learned. It may be impossible to say just how

4

Back to the City

Having spent four good years in this town, I left to fulfil my life's goal, which was to become a Jesuit priest. Jesuits run several schools around the world. I hoped that when I became a priest, I would also be a teacher in one of their schools.

After a short stint in a Jesuit seminary, I found that my lifelong ambition to become a member of the clergy was not what God wanted. I came home, unemployed and looking for a job. I answered an advertisement in the newspaper for a teacher at one of Sydney's private colleges, Waverley College, a boys' school. It was quite a long drive from home, but it was a job.

I found myself teaching Physics, Chemistry, Mathematics, Ancient History, Modern History, and Religion to fourth and fifth years (now Years 10 and 11) and Physics to third years (Year 9). The histories bothered me, as I had no academic grounding in either of them. However, I had a good grasp of the events of the current century and could spin a tale regarding World Wars I and II. I also found the subjects interesting. The Ancient History syllabus dealt with ancient Romans and Greeks, while the Modern History syllabus dealt mostly with the Napoleonic era up to World War I. I received a lot of help from regular teachers of the subject. I had no desk in the staffroom, which we visited only at recess for a cup of tea. All my preparation had to be done at home.

Despite the fact that I had three Science classes, I never once saw the inside of a Science laboratory. Science is a hands-on subject. It was this lack of experience that really detracted from the students' experience of

Science. I know that the school did possess at least one laboratory, but it was reserved for senior students only, presumably final-year students.

I was also given a rugby team to train. I had played rugby league at school, but rugby is somewhat different. I really was no help to the team. I supervised them while they trained themselves. I refused to attend the matches, which were on Saturday. I told the principal that my workload at this school was significantly more than I had experienced in my last school, so he allowed me the Saturday reprieve.

I found myself part of a small band of lay teachers. Some of the other teachers had had no training or experience, whereas I had been trained and had taught five years already. On the plus side was the free cooked lunch we got every day. We shared the lunch with the boarders.

I quickly found that the attitude of students toward teachers at the school was that the teachers were paid to serve them, somewhat as servants. They considered themselves to be a cut above the teachers.

Discipline in this college was administered by corporal punishment, in this case by the strap. I soon acquired one and proceeded to use it, fortunately rarely.

As the year progressed, I became more adept at history, due to the encouragement and advice of the regular teachers. I asked for and was allowed to purchase several books on the subject. Paid for by the college, these formed a small library on my desk which students could access. Whenever I set an assignment, I discussed the answers students handed in with experienced teachers before awarding any marks or comments.

Apart from the attitude many students had regarding teachers, behaviour of senior classes was good, with few problems. The senior students had a good attitude toward their studies, and I became used to teaching senior students, where I previously had taught mainly junior classes. The only problem was that I had no access to the laboratories. I was told that all necessary experiments would be undertaken in fifth year (Year 12) This meant that the Science I taught was purely academic. The supply of textbooks presented no problem, since students bought the necessary books either as new or second-hand from a student who had graduated.

Since the college was Catholic, I had to teach religion. This lesson was preceded by a prayer, the class standing up while the prayer was said. Students' desks accommodated two students, each with their own space under the lift-up desktop. The seat, however, was shared by both. One day, after the prayer, everyone being quiet, I asked the class to sit. Within seconds, one student started shouting, using the foulest of language. His message was "Get off my fingers!" The student had inadvertently reached back and had his fingers in between the two parts of the desktop hinge. His fingers were not broken, only bruised, but the solemn nature of the lesson had flown out the window.

I used to go into my classroom before school started to set things up and review the day's lessons. Occasionally, students came in and dropped their bags and books. While I was doing this one morning, a student who had come in decided to dust his desk by flicking a handkerchief over its surface. Unfortunately, there was a tiny piece of chalk on the desk, and straight as an arrow, it flew into my glasses, shattering one of the lenses. The headmaster gave me time off to get the glasses repaired, but I had to pay the expense. Neither the boy who had caused the accident nor the school offered to pay.

Examinations were held at the end of each term. There were three terms in the school year in those days. I was rostered to supervise examinations, as were all the teachers. Two tricks which I learned I never forgot. I was watching when one student ripped a page out of his writing pad, screwed it up, and threw it on the floor. A bit of rage at his mistake? I thought nothing of it until I saw another student pick it up. The penny dropped. I asked for the paper and inspected it: the complete answer to one question. Two reports to go in for cheating. The second trick I discovered when I saw a slip of paper appear, coming out of a hole in the wall between this class and the one next door, where students were doing the same examination. I grabbed this epistle just before the boy sitting next to this hole in the wall grabbed it. Again, the complete answer to a question. No report for cheating this time. I had beaten the recipient to the paper, and he luckily escaped; however, an enquiry later to the teacher who was supervising in the next classroom revealed the cheater, and a report followed.

During this year, I constructed my own telescope. It was a modified Coude six-inch reflector telescope based on the Newtonian plan. My brother, a qualified carpenter, made the tripod to my specifications, strong enough to support a telescope twice the size of the one I had planned. My brother's father-in-law, a metalworker, constructed the head of the telescope, a quite intricate job. I purchased a six-inch mirror made from a ship's porthole by a friend of mine who had made the mirror himself. Finally, I constructed the framework from aluminium girders purchased from the hardware shops. I had to purchase the eyepiece and assemble the telescope. After painstaking work, I had the perfect tool to further my studies of variable stars. The telescope went with me to my next appointment. After I retired, I donated it to a local Astronomy club.

While I was on the staff of that school, I traded my Morris Minor in and bought a Triumph Herald. It was car of the year but later proved to be, in some ways, a lemon. More later.

This school spent substantial amounts of money on promotion and advertising while paying its staff well under the current State school wages for teachers. Towards the end of term 2, I discovered that while a teacher with fake degrees was well paid, the untrained, unexperienced teachers and I were being paid much less. I rang up the DET and asked what the pay rate was for a teacher like me. I then approached the headmaster requesting a pay rise.

He asked how much, and I quoted the department's figure. "Oh no," he said. "You are asking too much."

I said, "I will thus resign at the end of the next school vacation."

He said, "You mean at the beginning of the vacation."

"No," said I. "I am entitled to be paid for that vacation."

And so he agreed. I rang up the DET, asking if there were any jobs for me. The officer who spoke with me asked if I could start straight away. I said that I could not but I could start at the beginning of the next term, and so it was that I received an appointment to another city school not so far from my home.

I cannot say that I enjoyed this episode in my career. I missed the collegiality of the public schools that I had taught in. I did not ask for the pay rise just to have an excuse to leave. I just felt that I was being dealt with unjustly. I did learn a lot about Ancient and Modern History, and I must say that I enjoyed that.

I know that other teachers in schools such as this one love the experience and do well. It was just not for me at that time. As you will see, I later became a teacher in another private boys' school. This was a much better experience and probably reflects what I had learned in the many years between these two experiences.

5

Coming of Age

My new appointment was a developing school, Cabramatta High. It was just three years old. It had been built as a twin school, one campus for boys and the adjacent one for girls. By the time the school was opened, government policies had changed, and it was decided to amalgamate the school into one co-ed school. I was given several junior Science classes, including two classes of students at the bottom end of the academic spectrum, who were a delight to teach. I also had a class of students who were being boarded at this campus while their new school buildings were being built.

At this stage, I was trying desperately to lose weight. My doctor gave me some pills to take. It was only when I came to the end of a bottle of these pills and swept the small amount of powder remaining into my mouth that I discovered just what the pills were. They were Dexedrine, a stay-awake stimulant often used by truck drivers who drove state to state. Now, I began to understand why I had become so busy at this school, initiating things and working long hours. Despite the pills, I came of age in this school, and the work ethic remained the same for the rest of my career.

One favourite demonstration I used in class involved the concept of air pressure. An old ruler or a thin strip of wood was placed on the front bench, with half of it protruding over the edge and a sheet of newspaper placed over the part which was on the bench. The trick in this demonstration is that if the part protruding from the newspaper, not under it, is given a sharp rap, it will break rather than tear through the paper. Air pressure on the newspaper is supposed to keep the paper firmly in place and the wood under it, causing the wood to break at the edge of the paper. All this was done without telling the class anything until after the demonstration.

I set it up and then administered the sharp rap. The ruler tore through the paper and flew straight down the room between white-faced students, finally hitting the back wall. I recall a sea of stunned faces, wondering, "What the hell did he do that for?" I was extremely lucky that I didn't hit anyone. I apologised profusely and explained what was supposed to happen. With everyone well clear, I repeated the demonstration, and it worked; the ruler broke, and the paper stayed intact.

On another occasion, I was demonstrating the difference between a physical change and a chemical change by mixing iron filings and sulfur in two test tubes, to one of which I added a small amount of acid. The mixture bubbled, and I showed that the gas produced was hydrogen by applying a flame to the mouth of the tube and observing the small explosion as the hydrogen gas exploded. The second tube was heated until it glowed red and was chemically changed. After this tube had cooled, acid was added, and bubbles were produced.

As usual when I did a demonstration, the class were sitting around the teacher's bench. I quickly took the tube around, inviting the students to take a gentle whiff. The gas produced was hydrogen sulfide, rotten-egg gas. I wafted the gas at the students so that they just got a small whiff. Unbeknown to me, a student had left his seat and came around behind me. He leant over and applied his nose to the tube and inhaled. He recoiled from the tube and looked faint, so I asked him to sit just outside the room for a few minutes until the experience passed. I thought that a little fresh air would clear him and that he would return, cured.

I thought no more until a messenger came from the office, saying that they had a student who was experiencing breathing difficulties and complaining that he was about to die from poisonous gas. It was the student I had sent outside. As it turned out, he had panicked and gone to the office, who had called the ambulance. The ambulance officers found that there was no damage, and the oxygen mask they were using was not connected to an oxygen bottle. The student was simply breathing air. One learns from experiences such as this.

My chart-making skills developed greatly, and I made quite a few, properly labelled and mounted.

When I started teaching, I had joined the National Science Teachers Association, an American body. They published an article showing how to build a display with a slide film projector and a prism to demonstrate refraction of light and the spectrum. I built the apparatus. This was much appreciated by the students, who could easily see the phenomenon. In later years, schools were issued kits which students could use to do the same thing.

Another experiment I did with a first-year (Year 7) class involved acids and alkalis and the use of litmus paper. I foolishly issued each small group of students a whole book of litmus paper. Of course, when equipment was returned, lots of litmus paper had been purloined. The Science master was not happy. Another valuable lesson learned.

Another incident reinforced in me that there are some things over which one had no control. I was doing the rotten-egg gas experiment for a class in a demonstration room when the class began to carry on, holding noses and complaining that they were being poisoned. The carrying on lasted a little while longer than it should have.. Instead of shouting at the class to behave, I let it go. I couldn't have stopped it, anyway. The class soon settled. It was a good joke, anyway.

The lower classes were a delight because, being small classes, the students had more individual attention, and they were so keen to learn. One day, I took the classes to a factory where they were making pressure tanks. We were dealing with air pressure, and the excursion would be a valuable learning experience. The process of making pressure tanks involved a lot of electric welding. Electric welding rods are discarded when they become too small. The excursion went well, and a report from the factory said that no one had to pick up all the discarded bits of welding rods after the day's work (the class has souvenired the lot).

Electricity lent itself to many interesting experiments. One of my favourites was to connect a chain of students to an induction coil. The first student in the chain held her finger to one terminal on the discharge terminal of the coil, while the students at the end of the chain held their finger on the other terminal. All this was done at the end of the lesson. As the bell sounded for change of periods, the switch key was momentarily pressed, activating the induction coil. A shock of electricity went through the entire class; all the girls screamed, and then everyone laughed and went onto the next class. The teachers of the next classes complained that some students seemed to be highly excited and took a long time to settle down. However, if I was still teaching, I would not do that again. I would have no idea how this could affect some students who could have heart problems. One could hardly ask students, "Who has a heart problem?"

Another electrical experiment involved the use of the Van der Graaf generator. A student would be asked to stand on a rubber mat while holding a hand to the globe on the top of the generator. As the generator developed a significant electrical charge, the student's hair would begin to stand up. This worked particularly well with girls with long hair. If students came up to the one standing at the generator and touched fingers, each would receive a little shock, and the hair would drop a little. Who said that Science is not fun? Once again, I have to admit that this experiment could be risky. I guess that I was lucky that no one was injured.

An excursion to the newly built Warrangamba Dam was organised near the end of the year, and I was picked to be one of the teachers to accompany the whole of Year 8. It had not been long since the dam, which supplies much of Sydney's water supply, had been built. The students found the site to be most interesting; however, as I recall, there was a suspension bridge over the spillway of the dam which tended to sway. Our students had a fine time making it sway more and more, until security staff called a stop to it. Some poor students became so terrified that they just hung on, not moving, but it provided a lesson in wave movement.

Passing a class being taught by a colleague one day, I heard him proclaiming loudly, "And it isn't shit; it's faeces."

Okay, I thought; *that is so.*

Some years later, I met the teacher and reminded him of that incident. He said that there was one little girl in a class several years later who asked him privately one day, "What are faeces?"

He pondered for a few seconds and thought, *Well, here goes*, and said, "Shit; do you know what I mean?"

She said, "Thanks, now I understand."

Because the school had been built initially as two schools, some of the rooms were quite a distance away from the others. On one day each week, I parked my car next to one room in which I taught so that I could dash out to the car and drive to the next room, arriving just before the next class arrived. Had I not done that, I would have arrived some minutes after the class had arrived.

Although I had only been at this school for one term, I had learned a lot and was ready to give the country another chance. I applied to go back to the country school where I had been, but I was appointed to Nyngan High. My Science master, who had some pull with the DET, got me an appointment in Tamworth which is not that far from Armidale where I was studying by correspondence from the University of New England.

Because the school was a developing school, there was a good, almost pioneering feeling in the staff and the students. There were few discipline problems.

I left that school feeling very pleased with myself and looking forward to another new life. I really felt that I had become a competent teacher .

6

Back to the Country

The transfer came through, and it was most satisfactory.

My first job was to contact the parish priest of Tamworth to see if he knew of anyone who would board a teacher. He found me one, and I corresponded with her. Yes, I could stay with her.

I had devised a lot of teaching aids in my year at home, and my packing was quite extensive. The six-inch reflector telescope I had built was going with me. I determined that I would travel to my country appointment by car, carrying as much of my worldly possessions as I could and sending the rest of them by train. I would get to my destination on Friday before school started and settle in.

Come Friday morning, and I set out. The journey was uneventful, taking seven hours. I found the address of my board and settled in. I drove to the high school to have a look around.

Tuesday morning was the day; up early, eat breakfast, pack the briefcase, and drive off to the new school. I met the deputy principal, who welcomed me and informed me that I should not have been there; my appointment had been changed. However, he said that he was going to keep me until the person who had the appointment showed up. She did, next day, and I taught one lesson during that first day.

I found out that the woman who got my appointment had been born in Tamworth. Her appointment was originally to Mudgee. She had spoken to the appointments officer in the DET, probably crying on his shoulder about how cruel the DET was, sending a beginning teacher to a place far away from her hometown. (Can you tell that I was not happy?) No problem; he swapped us. In those days, appointments were delivered by telegram. The telegram changing my appointment had been delivered on Saturday to my parents' home, one day after I had set out. My parents, having no phone, had no way of informing me of the change apart, from posting it in the mail. The telegram caught up with me at the school next day.

Naturally, I was both disappointed and furious with the department. When the woman replacing me arrived, I asked her if she had booked any accommodation in Mudgee. "Yes," she said, "with the Country Women's Association." This meant that I had nowhere to stay. The deputy principal freed me from any further obligations and advised me to pay a visit to the district inspector of schools. He was most sympathetic. He said that my expenses in moving to the new school would be paid by the DET; once I had rebooked my goods for the new train journey, I should set off to the new town, travelling during school hours, and if I was still on the road at school finishing time, I should book into a motel at the department's expense.

I set off and had a good trip. At school finishing time, I was ten kilometres from Mudgee, so I continued; the nearest motel was in that town anyway. It took me until nine o'clock that night until I found accommodation in a men's hostel.

The next day, I fronted up at the new school, explaining why I was four days late. I received my timetable and was introduced to the Science staff and the deputy principal. I also received a telegram from the DET, demanding why I was late taking up the appointment. I wrote a letter explaining in no uncertain terms why I was "late" and demanded that this telegram be removed from my file.

I never forgot to remind the DET of this muck-up. Each time I moved from one school to another, I had to provide a history of where I had taught. I always included Tamworth to which I had been appointed with the time served: "two days" (my little protest).

As it turned out, the time I served in this town was fruitful. The town itself was pretty, and the surrounding countryside was beautiful, but there was one problem: the people were not friendly. The town was stratified. Teachers belonged to the white-collar class along with bank employees and other professionals. Teachers were often itinerants, not expected to stay in the town too long. As I was preparing to leave Mudgee after three years' service, I was having a last drink in the golf club of which I was a member; a lady said to me that I hadn't mixed very well with people. I replied that she had never invited me to her house, and I certainly was not able to invite her to mine. She was right, to an extent. I had my nose in books much of the time, studying, but I had, in fact, mixed quite a lot, as you will see.

Mudgee, like many country towns, had a winery (it now has several). The wines were (and still are) very good. I had not drunk wine before and soon became to like it, although I never abused it. We were quite friendly with the owner of the winery and one night were invited to inspect his cellar. It was under the ground. Until that night, I had not known how good white wine could be. The town also had historical connection with one of Australia's famous poets, Henry Lawson.

Two of the tourist attractions of this town were the Catholic and the Anglican churches, each beautiful in its own way; the two of them faced each other across the town square.

After about a week, I found better accommodation with a lady who boarded teachers. She was a widow of a teacher and felt that by boarding teachers, she was doing her little bit. She was on the local town council and was very active in the Country Women's Association. She boarded two men (me included) and one woman. She used to cook our meals, do our washing and ironing, and make our beds. She even provided lunch for us. We would drive home for it.

We lazy people drove to school. Had we walked, it would have taken all of fifteen minutes. Our landlady was a very personable lady and a good cook. Her married daughter and family lived next door. We men had our shared bedroom in another house next door, owned by a man who worked at the local hospital as an odd jobs man. Our landlady looked after him, doing his washing and keeping an eye on him. Each night, he cooked his dinner, a boiled sausage. I don't think he ever washed the saucepan; it was encrusted with the fat of ages. Yuck. He had his other meals at the hospital.

In the front of our landlady's front garden was a fishpond, which also had a small family of frogs. One lazy Sunday afternoon, as I was out on the lawn, I happened to look into the pond. After telling Biology classes the mating habits of amphibians, there it was, unfolding right before me. So the textbooks were right, after all. Unfortunately for the future generations of frogs, a fish was there busily consuming the fertilised eggs as fast as they were released. Science teachers have to keep their eyes and ears open at all times.

In my third year, the man with whom I had shared the room for the past two years moved on, and another teacher took the room. He was such a snob that I couldn't stand a bar of him, so I went looking for another place to board. The lady who took me in was quite old. She had a few rules: no more than five shirts a week, and no burning the midnight oil. However, she used to feed me up to the extent that I couldn't eat all she served up. She really was a kind lady. We had a silent dispute in the way we made the bed. She arranged the bed cover one way, and I remade the cover my way every day.

One night, I put the battery for my camera' flash on charge. She complained that I was using too much electricity. The charging unit used a minute amount of electricity, so I presented her with threepence (about two and a half cents), saying that that is what is would cost her at the most. I went looking for another place to board, eventually finding one. This lady looked after me well and had no rules. Peace.

My Science classes were all in the junior school (Years 7–9), while my Maths class was in the senior school (Year 10). The subject was General Mathematics, and I coped very well. Fortunately, the students had textbooks, so I did not have to write everything on the board.

The Science staffroom was actually the laboratory's preparation room. We shared that room with big bottles of sulfuric acid and all sorts of poisonous chemicals. Other staffs had staffrooms with no nasties. The common room was, in fact, the staff study of the English and history staff. Everyone went there for morning tea each day. The principal issued instructions for the day and correspondence. I had tried to get a post office box, but there were none available, so I had all my mail addressed to the school. One correspondent from America used to address me as "Professor." The principal was slightly annoyed at this, but I enjoyed it.

I let it be known that I was a certified women's basketball umpire, so my sport became women's basketball. I became the coach of the school team, although I had no idea of tactics. If the school team had to travel to a match, I went with them. I also took over the job of official school photographer. At each big sporting event, I took black-and-white photographs. I printed them out, and the kids could order copies. In those days, one took the photos and took the exposed roll of film to the pharmacist, who sent it away for processing. It usually took a few days. I sent copies of my photos to the local newspaper, and they printed them.

Another job I took on was running school dances. We had one each month, and these were very popular with the kids. One popular dance for the adults was a Scottish "Strip the Willow." Part of the dance was to twirl the girl and hand her on to the next male. The principal would not allow us to have this dance. I think that he was afraid that the kids might see the girls' underwear.

I spent most of my spare time studying. I resumed my studies for a BA at the University of New England. I decided to do Pure Maths I. One of the Science teachers was studying university Maths, the same course that I had enrolled in. He was older than I, having been a navigator on Lancaster bombers in World War II. He had a DFC and had been a Flight Lieutenant. We helped each other.

We did several assignments during the year before sitting for the final exam. The two of us continued with the Maths course until we had completed the three years. We had weekly assignments to do and compared our answers before sending our assignments into the university. This was all before the computer age. Assignments were handwritten and went by post to the school.

Students studying externally had to complete and post their assignments in time to beat the deadline imposed on both internal and external students studying the same course. A representative of the external students took up the matter with the administration. Because it could take days for our assignments to reach the university, they sometimes arrived late, incurring a penalty. Our alternative was to post them in early. We thought that this was unfair because internal students doing the same course could hand in their assignments on the closing day. It was finally settled by having the university taking note of the date stamped on the envelope in which the assignment was posted and accept that this would represent the day the assignment was handed in.

Examinations from the university were generally held in our town in the Anglican church hall, supervised by the Anglican rector. During our first-year exam, I dozed off, bored to tears working out a matrix. When I woke up, I looked at the clock and went hell for leather to finish the exam. I received a merit grade for the exam and won five pounds for being the top external studies Maths student. In the second year, I did Pure Maths II and Education II. I passed both. In the next year, I studied Pure Maths III and passed. My friend reckoned that if we ever got through Maths III, we could call ourselves geniuses. So there you are, I am a genius.

In our yearly exam for Pure Mathematics III, the rector left us unsupervised while he attended to parish business. My fellow student asked me for the formula to do a calculation in one of the questions. I had to tell him that I had forgotten it, which was the truth. Had I remembered the formula, I would have told him the same; I do not like to cheat).

I joined the golf club, which had one of the prettiest courses in the state.

I was never any good playing golf, but I enjoyed it. I took a photograph of the eighteenth hole and entered a contest. When the tourist people produced a brochure advertising this town, the photograph I took was featured in it. I also played competition tennis in the lowest grade. I'm just not good at sports. I did, however, go to dances run by various organisations. I thought that I was a fair dancer. I even owned a pair of dancing pumps.

There were two big stores in town which sold everything. One of them, Loneregans, gave customers bingo tickets, one for each ten shillings (one dollar in today's money) spent. Each Monday night, the local radio station called the numbers, and people tuned in, marking their cards. A few of the teachers used to gather at our boarding place and pool their bingo tickets. One person sat on the phone, ready to ring up if we won. The first prize was to go to the first person to ring in with one complete line of numbers. One night, somebody did ring in. One of the numbers they mentioned was 13. Our people retorted that 13 had not been called. I rang the radio station and informed them of that fact. A commercial followed the award of this prize. After the commercial, calling the numbers resumed. No prize for guessing the first number which was then called.

The Catholic church had no youth club. Together with one of the young men in the parish, I set up a youth club, and we met every month to socialise and sometimes to dance. One of the young ladies in the club took a fancy to me, and a small romance developed. I told her once that I was driving back home to spend a weekend with my parents. She told me that she had been invited to attend a sales conference that weekend and asked if I would drive her to the city. This I did. Later, I found that there was no conference. Single male teachers are sometimes attractive to young ladies in country towns because they move on after a few years, and if the lady snares a teacher, she has her ticket out of town. I began to realise this and broke off the relationship. I believe that this situation also works in reverse.

I was often a guest for dinner of a couple who were teachers in the local technical college. One night, they also invited a nice young lady to dinner. It was obvious that they were trying to pair me off. I hated that, and their attempt came to nought.

The telescope I had made when I spent a year at home got some use. One night, while I was studying the moon, a bat flew across my view. Against the moon and magnified several times, the result was that I nearly had a heart attack. I had become interested in observing meteors and used to sit up at night, counting them and mapping their path through the sky. The observations were sent to the American Meteor Society. During this year, I was approached by AMS's director to become the Australasian director. I wrote a small book on meteor observing and had the appropriate maps of the sky cut onto stencils, which I used to reproduce the maps.

Early in my days at this school, I was teaching a Science class about air pressure. I was about to make a mercury barometer, but before I did, I decided to show the effect of a vacuum on a column of air in a glass tube, the lower end of which dipped into mercury. I connected a long glass tube to a vacuum pump, using a rubber tube. As I turned the handle of the pump, the mercury rose, but not evenly. It began to bob up and down. Eventually, as the mercury rose higher and higher, it went right through, into the pump. The mechanism of the pump was made of brass, and mercury amalgamates with brass. I received a reprimand from the Science master, as the pump had to be sent to the city for repair.

For the first time, I had good access to a laboratory. I demonstrated some lessons, but at every opportunity, I had the students do their own experimentation. To make the demonstrations more interesting, I had the class gather around the teacher's bench on stools and even sitting on front benches. The students appreciated this, and I believe that some developed a real love of Science. The workbook the students used to record their Science notes had ruled lines on the left-hand page with a graph page as the right-hand page. Since students were expected to draw the apparatus, we developed their art skills, as well.

I had read an article in a magazine from the National Science Teachers Association which described a method of projecting water waves using an overhead lamp; students could see interactions between the waves and barriers. This experiment required a ripple tank, a glass-bottomed shallow tank of water. The school did not have one. I purchased a sheet of glass and some timber to make a ripple tank, billing the school. Because I had not spoken to the principal before buying the materials, I was given a short lecture. However, the demonstration worked beautifully.

For as long as I can remember, experiments on gases had as their aim "to prepare and examine the properties of such-and-such gas." I think that while I was at this school, the edict went out that aims of experiments had to be in the form of a question, like "How is such-and-such a gas prepared, and what are its properties?"

One day, I was demonstrating how to make hydrogen gas. The

experiment was, in the new parlance, how is hydrogen gas prepared, and what are its properties? The usual method involved adding dilute hydrochloric or sulfuric acid to zinc (if a quicker result was desired, magnesium could be substituted). The hydrogen could be collected either over water or by downward displacement of air. To hurry things along a bit, I applied some heat. The result was that the top blew off the apparatus, hitting the ceiling (fortunately, not hitting anyone and not splashing anyone with the chemicals involved). The students who had been gazing out the window missed all the fun, enquiring, "What happened?" From that day, I had rapt attention whenever I did a demonstration.

Students loved preparing hydrogen and collecting it in inverted empty test tubes. They could then, lighted match in hand, turn the test tube up the right way, allowing a little air to mix, and apply the flame to the side of the top of the test tube. The resounding "pop" delighted them, and it was hard to restore order after a session.

After preparing some gas jars of carbon dioxide in another lesson, I poured the invisible gas down a specially prepared slope towards a small lit candle. The students were delighted when the candle was extinguished by the invisible gas which, as they saw, did not support combustion. After doing their own experiments to make oxygen, the students were also delighted when their glowing wooden splints burst into flames when lowered into the oxygen they had made.

While the class were busy answering some questions, I set about connecting an induction coil to some vacuum tubes. I was getting ready to demonstrate cathode rays. While I was doing this, a student approached the front bench where I was working and stood passively, awaiting my preparations before speaking. The power to the induction coil was controlled by a press switch and was off. He waited until he saw that I had my two hands shorting the coil when he reached out and hit the switch. I rarely if ever swear in class, but that day …

At the end of my first year, I prepared a Maths examination paper for my general Mathematics class. The examination consisted of two parts. The first part was multiple choice, to be handed in after one hour, and the second part, consisting of calculations and writing, went for another two hours. At the end of the first hour, I collected the first part and marked it. I prepared a list of students and their marks and put it on the notice board. Shortly after the exam finished, it was reported that several girls were going about crying. They were from my class and did not like the mark they received. Banned: no publishing of exam results until all exams finished was the edict from the deputy principal.

The Science Department received a new glass-fronted cupboard and engaged a local carpenter to fix it to the wall in the laboratory. The Science master stored all our electric meters, ammeters, milliammeters, and voltmeters in the cupboard. Storing the equipment in this way made it a lot easier to access, and it made a nice display. One day, two of us were in the staffroom chatting when we heard a series of crashes coming from the laboratory. After a few seconds, we rushed to investigate. The cupboard was slowly coming off the wall, spilling its contents of valuable meters, with the Science master slowly sinking to the floor under the weight of the cupboard. A call to the carpenter and some nasty words sorted that problem out.

One job I had was to prepare dilute solutions of the acids. We had no laboratory attendants, having to do all those things ourselves. I should have known better, but when I had emptied a large bottle of sulfuric acid, I decided to wash out the bottle. With a huge crack, the bottom fell out of the bottle, fortunately into the sink. My lesson: when diluting sulphuric acid, pour the acid into the water, not the water into the acid.

In my second year at this school, the DET decided that they would finally introduce the Wyndham scheme, which had been talked about for years. We had studied it in college six years before, and now here it was. Instead of three years leading to the Intermediate Certificate (at the end of the third year, or Year 9) followed by another two years of secondary schooling, leading to the Leaving Certificate (end of fifth year, Year 11), the new scheme consisted of four years leading to the School Certificate and another two years for the Higher School Certificate. Henceforth, first year was to be called first form, up to the sixth form. Several years later, first form became Year 7 and sixth form became Year 12. Big advances in education?

New courses were introduced, all without any preparation of textbooks and very little in the way of guidance. The curriculum for the first year of Science included Astronomy and Geology. We all had to bone up on the new material. We were fortunate in that the Science master had studied Geology, and the town was in a geological part of the state that had samples of all the rocks which had to be studied. Before long, we had multiple samples of various kinds of volcanic, metamorphic, and sedimentary rocks. I was the Astronomy expert and passed my knowledge on to the others.

Within a month or so, a group of Science masters in Sydney (Edmonds, Hughes, and Kahn) had produced a slim textbook for the new course.

Later came the textbook which became known as the Messel, named after a professor of Physics at Sydney University who had supervised the production of the book. He had assembled a group of teachers, including two of the teachers who had taught me at Teachers College and one who had taught me at school, to write material for the new book. We received three pilot edition books at the school. They acted as a source for the new curriculum.

In one class, I had a boy who was a real thorn in the side of several teachers. In class, he was a great disturbance. He disrupted classes by refusing to do the assigned work. In my class, we came to an agreement: He could sit down at the back of the class and read his comics or other things, so long as he did not disturb the class. Occasionally, on his own volition, he would come to sit near the front of the class, behaving himself and answering questions, but eventually, he would become bored again and return to his seat at the back of the room. After I left the school, I heard that he'd been arrested for stealing a car (he was fourteen) and driving it some three hundred miles away to Newcastle.

The teacher who taught Biology also taught Agriculture. The school had a small plot where various crops were grown. It was quite a popular subject. One day, he returned home to find his wife had committed suicide. This shook us all. We knew his wife and had no hint that she was depressed. Depression is much discussed today, but then, no one knew much about it. The teacher applied for a transfer at the end of that year. Later, I heard that he had remarried and was making a success of his life.

One task all teachers had was to mark the roll in a special period each day. I used a fountain pen and bought some special ink: teal blue. In no time flat, the principal had me on the carpet for using green ink in the roll.

"Only accountants use green ink," he said.

"But the ink was blue," said I. I now know what colour teal is. After arguing, I eventually apologised and got myself a different colour of blue ink.

While I was at this school, the DET decided to introduce counsellors into schools. We welcomed the man but were rather suspicious and recommended that he see Marcia, a girl who was giving everyone problems. He interviewed her, and we invited him to join us at the local hotel after school for a drink. We asked him how he found Marcia.

"A good kick in the ringy, dangy doo [Australian slang for bottom] would do her the world of good," he said.

"Have another beer," I said. "You're one of us."

One day, I was running late for playground duty. I swung through the door leading to a flight of stairs, missed the top one, and tumbled down the steps. As I uttered my favourite expletive, I noticed a small group of girls sitting on the bottom step. When I finished my flight, I noticed that the girls were nowhere to be seen. I got a sprained ankle and a day off school out of that one.

One girl in my class suffered a severe attack of peritonitis and died as a result. The whole class, the principal, and I attended the funeral. The minister gave such a sermon that was a real dirge. As the coffin was being lowered into the grave, one girl became hysterical. The principal could not shake her out of it, so he slapped her. That did it. I sometimes wonder how that would go in the present time.

The school had a cadet unit. One day, they were doing rifle drill. I couldn't resist it. Having been a member of the drill platoon in my national service not that many years ago, I borrowed a rifle from one of the cadets and demonstrated just how to do it. That made me feel good. Each year, the cadets staged a passing-out parade. A major general, an old boy of the school, was invited to take the salute. I drove the principal's car with the principal and the general onto the parade, where they were ceremoniously received by the senior cadet underofficer. Very swish. When I did my national service in the army, that general's son was in my company.

The students at this school were a mixed lot, a few coming from surrounding farms but most living in the town. There were a few discipline problems, but on the whole, students were well behaved and many had good ambitions to go on to further studies. The town had a technical and further education (TAFE) college. University study by correspondence was available, and jobs were plentiful both in the town and in the surrounding farms. I believe that I had a good influence on the students. After I left the school, some students used to correspond with me.

After three years at the school, I decided that I wanted to move on. I applied for the move and at the end of the year packed up and went home, all this before I had received a new appointment, so that I did not officially leave the school. After leaving this school, I did not teach Mathematics until my last permanent appointment.

When I come to think of it, I did a lot of things in that town and learned a lot. I was ready for a change.

7

Back to the City Again

This appointment was most interesting. North Sydney Boys High is a selective school for boys. These were the brightest boys from that area of the city. Aspirants to this school had to sit for a special examination in their final year of primary school.

I found out that I was replacing a Science teacher who had gained entry to the school during the Christmas holiday and had gassed himself to death. I was asked if I wanted to sit at his old desk. I had no problem.

Once again, my staffroom was a preparation room to a laboratory. I was placed in charge of this laboratory. My lab was in really bad shape. It was a very old-fashioned laboratory, with two long benches running the full length of the room. Students sat at either side of the bench, facing each other. Along the backs of the sinks was a divider with shelves, presumably for chemicals, and exposed plumbing running along the top of the shelving. There were several sinks and taps for water and gas. The sinks drained into tubs filled with marble chips (when I began at the school, they were also filled with rubbish, consisting of discarded pens, paper, and broken glass). The marble chips prevented solids from entering the plumbing and helped to neutralise the acids.

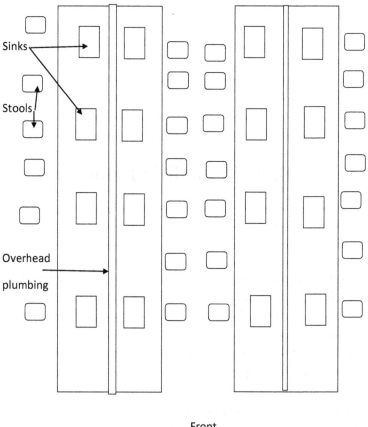

Front
of
Laboratory

I set about removing the rubbish, which was clogging the drains in the sinks. I did a thorough clean of the bench tops and the plumbing. The preparation room was also a mess. The chemicals and apparatus in the preparation room were in disarray, so I proceeded to clean it all up. I cleaned out each sink, threw out empty bottles and old chemicals, and restocked the prep room so that one could find one's way around. The Science Master was most impressed.

My desk was alongside the prep room. My confrere in this mini staffroom was a veteran of the Korean police action. He was a firm disciplinarian; I witnessed him one day disciplining his class by placing a watch glass with a little butyric acid in it in an open window, where the breeze would waft the smell (like rancid butter) into the classroom. The boys sat there, grim faced, vowing secretly to either kill this teacher or pick up their act.

Our little neck of the woods was a short distance from the rest of the school, being attached to it by means of a walkway. There was a small alley next to it, which was very convenient for parking. There were newer laboratories at the other end of the school. I taught one of my classes in one of these laboratories. The rest of my lessons were taught in my domain or in ordinary classrooms (there are never enough laboratories in any school).

On the day I began teaching at this school, a new principal started. He did two things right away: He decommissioned a classroom and declared it a common room, ordering appropriate furniture. His second thing was to say that he would make the school top of the state. He did that. By the end of the year, the school had achieved that distinction.

My roll class was 3E (Year 9). The classes were graded according to achievement. That meant that the boys in my class were bottom of the heap. One day, I copied the IQs of the class from their pupil record cards and averaged them. Their average was 119. Not bad for bottom of the heap.

One of my classes was Form 5 (Year 11) Biology. I hadn't taught Biology before, but I had done Botany I at Sydney University. One of the students was taking Biology honours. Fortunately for me, this student had a girlfriend in Norh Sydney Girls High who was doing the same course. I remembered enough from my previous studies to be able to help.

I set about teaching the Biology class. Sometimes, the Honours student helped answer questions in class, and fortunately, I knew enough Biology to fill in. What he didn't know, I knew. He did well in his examinations at the end of the year.

The Science master was Anthony Edmonds, one of the authors of Edmonds, Hughes, and Kahn fame. I nearly blotted my copy book with him in a lesson I taught about electrical resistance. His laboratory had 240V AC power points and 12V DC points. The latter were powered by a car battery in the preparation room. I connected one resistor to the 12V and promptly blew it up. It just couldn't take the current. The resistor had to be sent in for repairs. Tony wasn't perturbed. He simply said that in future, I should use the 1.5V telephone batteries that we had in the store.

One day, when the class was experimenting with chemical solutions, they came to the final clean-up. At this stage, we had no laboratory attendant, so the boys had to clean the test tubes, wipe down the benches, and so on. One bright spark decided that, for fun, he would fill a test tube with water and throw it into his neighbour's face. The neighbour decided to retaliate, but the test tube he grabbed still had caustic soda in it, and it got into the first boy's eyes. A quick trip with me taking the victim to the hospital, where they washed out his eyes (we had already tried that) and declared that no damage had been done. All this mayhem had happened in seconds.

As part of the course, we took an excursion to visit a rock platform by the sea. In the process, we collected some specimens and brought them back to school to be preserved the next day. The day of the excursion was a Thursday. I was sick on the following day, so the specimens sat in a cupboard until Monday. When I opened the door to that cupboard on Monday morning, the smell nearly knocked me over. The specimens we collected never did get preserved.

Teaching students at this school was most challenging. The questions they asked and the answers they gave to my questions were way above what I had experienced in previous schools. It challenged me to keep up with my studies.

One day, a very special event was held. It involved special visitors and speeches, and the staff were asked to present themselves in academic dress, if they had it. One of our staff had a Master's degree from the Sorbonne in Paris (she was an instantaneous translator of language at government conferences). Her outfit outshone any of the others. I, of course, at that stage, had none because I had not graduated from university. When the classes lined up to go into the hall for the big event, one of the boys commented that I was not wearing my "Superman outfit."

Alas, not all the classes fitted into the hall, and my class was one that would not fit. The students were crestfallen. I was invited to go into the hall to sit with the staff but said that if my class couldn't go in, then neither would I. The boys much appreciated that. As compensation, they were formed into a guard of honour to the dignitaries who were leaving after the big event.

Being so old, the school still had some very old furniture. One day, new desks and chairs arrived and were promptly installed in some rooms. I happened to be passing one of these rooms to see one of the boys raising a brand-new chair over his head, ready to smash it on a new table. I soon put a stop to that. I guess that some people just cannot stand being around nice things. They just have to destroy. I compare this incident to the graffiti "artistry" I see today.

I applied for an inspection that year and was successful in getting on to List 1. This list was nothing more than a stepping stone to a further inspection for List 2, which enabled one to become a subject master or mistress.

Partway through the year, I decided to trade in my old car and get another car, a second-hand one with automatic transmission. This, however, was not the big event of the year. I reconnected with a girl who had been my girlfriend ten years before and began taking her out in the new car. After two weeks, I proposed; she accepted, and we became engaged.

That year, I became aware of the Royal Astronomical Society and learned how to join it. I received an invitation to join and became a Fellow of the Royal Astronomical Association (FRAS). Not quite as good as being a Fellow of the Royal Society (FRS), but at least some letters I could put after my name.

The first School Certificate examinations were held that year, and I applied to become a marker. I was accepted. Science exams were marked at the old showground in Sydney. The supervisor of marking had no idea of how long it would take, so he gave the markers the option of marking for five hours with a fifteen-minute break for dinner, paying us the princely sum of three pounds (six dollars) per hour. Normally, markers worked for four hours with an hour's break in the middle, and the pay was more appropriate. Because the school was some distance from the marking centre, it was necessary to leave school immediately after the bell and drive to the centre.

This school had been a challenge, and I had to be on my toes to keep up with the knowledge required. The students were so bright that I had to be at least one step in front of them (if not several steps). My love of teaching had gone up, and now I believed that I could use some managerial skills.

I heard that one of the men who had been at Teachers College with me had secured a position as relieving Science Master in another school. I applied for such a position, and with recommendation of my Science master, I received a promotion at the end of the year to a girls' high school as relieving Science master.

8

Girls, Girls, Girls

After ten years of teaching, I had been promoted, if only on a relieving basis. Wiley Park Girls High School had not had a head of the Science department for a couple of years, and they were glad to get one. I duly took leave of my boys' school for a girls' school. The principal offered me two choices of a staffroom: either in with the mistresses or in a Science preparation room. I opted for the latter. I was one of three men on the staff. One of them had the distinction of being part of a crew of a bomber in World War II; he had been forced to take to a parachute when his aeroplane had been hit. He wore the distinctive silkworm badge on his lapel.

I fitted in well with the staff, who were delighted when I announced that I was to marry during the term vacation. They asked me what I would like as a wedding present. I asked my fiancée what she wanted, but she said I should choose something useful for me. I told the staff that I wanted some tools and gave them a list. In the end, they gave me the money, and I purchased the tools.

The principal was one of the old-style educators. She made all the girls wear hats and gloves to school. If they ever went out of the school on an excursion, not only did the girls have to be properly attired, the women staff had to wear a hat. I once took a group of senior girls to meet Professor Julius Sumner-Miller at nearby Roselands shopping complex. I had to be chaperoned by a female member of staff.

The principal had strict ideas about the appearance of the students. One girl turned up one day having dyed her hair peach colour. Assisted by two of the mistresses, the principal washed the colouring out of the girl's hair over a sink in the Domestic Science department. I wonder how that would be accepted by today's parents and the DET.

The last act of each day was a roll call of all classes. Being a subject head, I did not have a roll class. One day, I was asked to leave the school at the beginning of roll call. I wondered what that was about and asked one of the staff the next day. The principal had had an inspection of the girls' underpants. Girls wearing black received a severe warning. I must say that black seems to be the colour of choice these days, not that I have done any inspections (I have two daughters).

At the end of the year, when marking HSC examinations began, I had a long way to travel and was anxious to leave. Because I had no roll call, I usually left early, until the principal found out. I was told not to leave until the bell rang. So I used to get into the car and sit inside the back gate with the motor running, until I heard the bell. I usually got to the marking centre on time.

I got on well with the principal, probably because I headed the Science Department, and she had been a Science teacher, but I was careful not to cross her. She held regular staff meetings; the staff stood on her arrival at the meeting and waited until she sat before they did.

After each whole-school examination session, each roll teacher had to prepare the results on departmental student results forms, to be presented to the principal. The forms recorded all the results in the previous examinations in all subjects for all the girls in the teacher's roll class. Means had to be calculated and recorded. The principal meticulously inspected each form, adding up marks and calculating means, before calling for the teacher who had prepared the form to discuss errors and omissions. I wondered how she found the time.

Every mistress (or master) had a role. Mine was that I oversaw ordering and replacing all furniture. In some cases, that meant that I was the one who had to move it, the piano included. I was also placed in charge of examination supervision rosters. As in many schools, examinations of all classes were held at mid-year and at end of year. I had to make sure that all examinations were submitted to the ancillary staff for printing on time and set up the timetable and the supervision roster; it was a big job.

Mistresses were not to be put on the supervision roster. This meant that fewer staff was available to supervise exams. Teachers were to supervise in a room for no more than one period. This meant that chains of supervision were inevitable. A had to relieve B, B had to relieve C, and C had to relieve

D. If you were unlucky in your planning, you had C having to relieve A. Then nobody moved. Sometimes, D would not be relieved until ten minutes had passed.

Once I was given an assistant to help. Unfortunately, she did not know about the restriction and rostered the mistresses on. This went on for one day, after which I was confronted by the principal, who wanted to know who had done the rostering. I said that the timetable was my responsibility and that it was my fault. She knew of course that my assistant had in fact rostered the day. Subsequent days had to be re-rostered.

The Science Department had its own supply of film strips. Some bright person in the past had decided that the place to house them was in the corridor to the ladies toilet. This, of course, was out of bounds for me, so if I wanted a particular film strip, I had to get to school early or ask one of the ladies to get it for me.

The school also had a supply of Messels (see chapter 6). They resided in two big boxes. The boxes had handles and could be accessed by two girls carrying a box. There were enough of the books to be able to issue one book between two, but only two classes could use them at a time. There were other textbooks, and these were in class sets, usually one class set of each textbook. At the end of the year, subject heads had to submit a list of what textbooks they would like the school to buy for the next year. The principal discussed these lists with the appropriate subject heads and placed the orders as she saw fit and as the school could afford.

Photocopying was just coming into vogue. At first, only the principal used it, and I was the one who had to produce the copies. The first photocopies were produced by a wet process; a stencil was produced by exposing a new stencil together with the original to a lamp, which was part of the equipment. All this had to be done in a darkened room. One then had to wait for the copies to dry. I became most proficient at this. I had to use the photocopier to produce examination rosters and notices that the principal wanted to go on several notice boards.

As the technology improved, stencils were no longer wet, and once again, I was the one to produce the copies. Still later, photocopiers assumed much the same technology as used today. It was interesting work, and at last, teachers could do their own copying.

Each year, all departments submitted their requests to the DET for the following year. Part of this request was for the supply of regular Science equipment such as beakers, flasks, and so on. Heads of Science departments in schools always ordered much more than they knew they were going to get. One year, I asked for ten microscopes. I got two. The next year, I ordered eight. I got two.

Part of the process was to count the number of items that the school possessed and to report that number. I used to farm the counting out to the Science teachers, so that one teacher had to count all the beakers and flasks, while another might have to count all the Bunsen burners. I called into a laboratory one day to find one of my teachers with lines of corks covering the front desk. He thought that we needed to know the exact numbers. I said that a good guess would be enough. A friend of mine from another school used to sweep all of the glassware into a garbage bin and report that he had none.

In due time, the orders (whatever the DET thought we should get) arrived. Initially, I recruited girls to carry the equipment upstairs (the laboratories were all upstairs). The edict came out from the principal: No girls to carry. I had to do the lot.

Liquid ink was regularly used by some of the girls, and inevitably, some of it got on their skirts. Someone's job was to make up the ink using powders and water. My job was to get it off with a special fluid. This I used to do with the girl standing in the middle of the corridor in full view of everyone, with me trying to sponge it off (can't have a male teacher doing that in the privacy of his staff study).

After the Russians put Sputnik into orbit, Western countries panicked. A special committee was set up by the DET to supply schools with extra Science equipment. The schools had no say in what they wanted. The committee decided that, so we began to receive all this special equipment, such as an overhead projector (to the envy of the other staffs in the school), an episcope, power packs, and so on. These arrived on a regular basis, sometimes being delivered to the wrong department in the school, entailing me having to rescue them because a delivery note accompanied each one. This went on for some years.

In due course, the annual swimming carnival came along. No male teachers were to attend; we stayed at school and did something useful. Goodness knows why. Maybe we would have shameful thoughts seeing the girls in their one-piece suits. Yes, no two-piece. Everyone had to have a one-piece suit, so I was told.

Mistresses and masters did not attend sport, but one day, there were so many staff absent through illness that I was called on to take some of the girls to basketball. I told the girls that I would umpire the game, and they thought they would get away with breaking the rules. I pulled up one player in the first minute of the game for an infraction. Little did they know that I had my umpire's certificate. From then on, they played to the rules.

I was rostered on playground duty. Some of the little minxes decided that they would try to embarrass me, as only girls can, so that it became hard to know where to look. Soon, however, the little game fell away. One day, there was a rush of girls to the back fence of the playground. I joined the rush. A pervert exhibitionist was the focus of their attention. He quickly disappeared when I hove into view.

Some of the girls who travelled to the school by train said that there was a regular exhibitionist by the side of the railway line. One afternoon after school, the principal took me with her to the railway station, where another one had been reported. He was long gone by the time we got there.

One morning after the weekend, the school was greeted by the sight of every copper drainpipe carrying rainwater from the roof having been stolen. Copper fetched an excellent price at the scrap yards. In due course, the drainpipes were replaced with galvanised iron pipes.

Getting back to the fact that the principal was a Science teacher: She once gave me a teaching aid she had used. In consisted of the element of a toaster, unravelled into one long strip. The idea was that you suspended the strip across the room and connected the two ends to the power (240V). When you switched on, the strip became instantly red hot and expanded, sagging down. It was a wonderful demonstration but highly dangerous. I tried it once before disposing of it.

The girls, particularly the senior girls, were a joy to teach, and we got on well. One of them was one of the best three Physics student I had ever taught. I met another girl several years later, when I had to see a physiotherapist. She was the physiotherapist and greeted me with, "I have waited a long time to inflict some pain on you." She was joking, but she was very bright. Another girl at this school became the state ombudsman. I taught some very bright girls. As I write this, I am preparing to attend a fiftieth anniversary of the time when these girls finished school. I am looking forward to attending the function.

Whenever I had to demonstrate anything, I invited the class to move to the front of the room and sit on the benches to get a better view. The first time I asked senior girls to do that, I had a complete display of "witch's britches" (these were frilly underpants then in fashion). I shaded my eyes, and after a laugh, the girls got the message. On another occasion, I was demonstrating cathode rays. I mentioned that the apparatus emitted some X-rays. Almost the entire class decamped to the back of the room.

One of the experiments in the senior Chemistry Messel was to make aluminium chloride by passing chlorine gas over aluminium powder in a long glass tube which was being heated. The equipment was difficult to set up, and in the end, I had two senior girls holding the ends of the glass tube while I applied heat to the tube containing the aluminium powder. Nothing happened for some time, but then, with a blinding flash of light, the aluminium turned instantly into aluminium chloride. I don't know which was whiter, the flash or the look on the faces of the two girls holding the tube as it happened. Nobody was hurt, and the girls, to their credit (or maybe because they were frozen with fear), did not let go of the equipment. They were as shocked as I was. I never repeated that experiment.

Ever since the day I began teaching, hooking up electrical apparatus such as resisters, switches, and various meters had to be done using thin fabric covered copper wire. Reels of it were supplied to schools. Reeling it out and connecting it up became a nightmare in complicated setups, so I devised a strategy to make things simpler: I coiled the wire around a pencil and bent each end into a hook so that it could be easily connected to the next piece of apparatus. The coil allowed the wire to be stretched out to the required length and later be pushed back and stored away, ready to be used again.

As more modern electrical apparatus was issued, sockets appeared, and it became apparent that if we had a supply of stout, flexible leads with plugs on either end, connecting up circuits would be a lot easier. I began ordering in plugs and leads and making up my own when the DET put such leads on the requisition forms. I ordered lots.

I requested an inspection that year. While the inspector was sitting in on my classes, he came into the laboratory as the class was carrying out an experiment where they placed a lit candle on a cork base, floating in a large bowl of water with a bell jar covering it (it's hard to explain the experiment to all but fellow Science teachers). However, once the girls had done the experiment, questions began to come in, such as, "What if we used two candles?" and "What if we used a bigger or smaller jar?"

Before long, there were girls all over the laboratory, getting equipment and doing their own little experiments. The inspector chose that moment to enter the laboratory and was greeted with a cacophony of noise as the girls went about their business. The inspector demanded to know if this noise was typical of my teaching. I explained that the girls were, in fact, doing Science, and who was I to stop that? He thought about that for a few seconds and agreed that they were, in fact, doing Science, and he moved on. I believe that I received a plus on that observation.

The end of my three years at this school came when the DET, having advertised the position of Science mistress each year (I was only relieving), finally had an applicant for the position. The principal retired at the same time, and she gave a present to every member of staff. She was a rock hound, and the present she gave me was a pen mounted on a polished sliver of rock.

I believe that I did well at this school. I received another appointment as teacher in charge of Science at a developing high school closer to my home, Kirrawee High. I would have cheerfully stayed at that school, but the DET decided that I would be useful elsewhere. It had been a useful and enjoyable experience, and once again, I had learned a lot.

9

A Developing School

My next school, Kirrawee High had only been in operation for three years. A few permanent masters and mistresses had been appointed. Once again, I was in a temporary position. I was the relieving Science master. The principal considered me as being equal to the permanent heads of departments and gave me full authority. I held this position for a year. At the end of the year, a permanent Science master was appointed, and I was then on my way to another school.

The ambience of the school was great. There was a pioneering spirit in the staff and the students. They were going to make a great school. The school had been built on what was called the "doughnut" scheme. Each building consisted of two storeys, in the shape of a square, with a courtyard in the middle. Each block was separate and was locked; this meant that every room was open to the outside and had a locked door. It was not unknown for teenagers to climb up the outside of the building and gain access to the inside. The only problem was that they had to exit the same way. In later years, the locking system changed so that once inside, one could simply open the gate and leave. This was a safety measure.

When this school was built, enough classrooms were built for the time when the school had a full complement of students. That meant that some of the rooms, including two laboratories, were left vacant. In any case, the Science equipment for these laboratories had not been delivered.

My staffroom housed a full range of subject teachers, including the English master. As the school developed, staffrooms would usually accommodate teachers of one subject. The staff was friendly and felt that they were pioneers.

Students here were very keen to learn, so it was a pleasure to teach them. Even though the school was in the development phase, there was some talk about expanding, demolishing a few more houses and using the land.

During this year, local government elections were held. I volunteered to be one of the officials to supervise the polling booths on the Saturday of the election. As a trial, the council decided that voting was not compulsory. Up until that time, voting for all citizens was mandatory. The result was that not many of those eligible to vote actually voted. The trial was a failure, and in future elections, voting was once again compulsory. Subsequently, I volunteered to become an official in state and federal elections and served as such for thirty-five years. I enjoyed it. After the first few years, I became the officer in charge, a position I held until I decided to retire when I reached the grand old age of seventy.

One week, I announced to all classes that we would be staging an astronomy night at the school. I had my own telescope and a four-inch telescope supplied by the DET. Many children came with their parents; others came by themselves, and I had asked one of the female members of the Science Department to attend. I invited her to our home for dinner. She asked if that would be inconvenient for me. I replied that my wife would "throw another spud into the stew." This expression, coming from Ireland, I believe, simply meant that we could provide for her, no trouble. She confessed to me later that she was not very happy because she hated stew. We didn't have stew, anyway. The night went well, and it was memorable for lots of kids.

Inspectors were always poking their noses into schools. During one inspection, an inspector found himself on the walkway in front of upstairs classrooms when the bell rang for recess. He was instantly surrounded by students hurrying in both directions, some at speed, to get to the school canteen before anyone else. He reported this to the principal as a complaint.

I was given the task of constituting one-way collision-free pathways for upstairs rooms. So up went the signs on walls upstairs. Being a mathematician, I decided that students would revolve around the doughnuts in a positive direction (anticlockwise for you non-mathematicians.) This meant that in some cases, students had to walk right around the doughnut just to get to the classroom next door, but there would be no more collisions with roaming inspectors.

Science departments do accumulate a lot of official paper, and there was nowhere to put it. After a conversation with a Science master of another school, I approached my principal to buy a filing cabinet and files. This upset him a little because no other department heads had ever made such a request. After I tried to buy a second-hand filing cabinet (must save money), a new one was bought, and files were filed.

That year, a large bushfire developed and was threatening nearby suburbs, including where I lived. One day, I kept popping out to the back of the school to look towards my suburb to see how the fires were progressing. In one of these looks, I could see large clouds of smoke issuing from my suburb. I gathered my stuff and informed the principal that I was leaving immediately to go home. He agreed. I went home and joined in the firefighting.

I tried my hose at home, but there was very little water pressure. Together with one of my neighbours, I set out to join a bush fire brigade. We found one and were issued with backpacks fitted with a pump and hose. Most of the time, we were involved in putting out rubbish fires. After doing this a while, we were moved to some new houses which were in danger of the fire. My friend and I were set the task of hosing down the trees in the path of the fire. Just before the fire reached us, it was, "Drop your hose and hide inside a newly built car garage." It was a close call. The fire crowned and jumped over us.

I am just too innocent, I guess, but there was an affair going on in my staffroom, and I was totally ignorant of it. One of the English teachers used to stay back after school with the English master. I thought that she was discussing what she was teaching, and that was that. I wasn't staying back after school so was not witness to the goings-on. However, it was none of my business. I only wish that someone had told me before I left the school.

During this year, the Teachers Union called a strike. It was the first time a strike had ever been called by the Teachers Union, and it was over pay. I never believed that teachers should go on strike. The principal pleaded with me to go on strike, but I held out. As a concession to members of staff who did go on strike (all of them did), I went to school but did not sign the sign-on book. So, officially, I was registered as being on strike.

After someone was appointed to be the permanent Science master, I applied to move to another school. Some of the students (girls) became quite upset because in their brief time at the school, no other teacher had left, and I guess they must have liked me or my teaching or whatever. They gave me a few small presents. I found the year to be a very pleasant experience.

10

Lab Attendants

In being posted to Caringbah High School, I was back to the ranks, as it were. After four years of overseeing Science departments, I was just an assistant teacher.

Hallelujah, this school had a Science attendant. I had been teaching fourteen years, preparing my own equipment, washing up, and so on, and now I could call on a Science attendant. Before coming to this school, the woman who was our attendant had worked as a Science attendant in a university, so she knew what she was doing. The Science teachers of the state had been lobbying for Science attendants for as long as I could remember, and finally the government had listened.

An innovation this year was the introduction of year advisors. These positions were paid at a higher rate, and the advisors even had their own offices (two to an office.)

On the first day of the school year, the first formal activity was the staff meeting. The staff put forward a request for male staff to be able to wear shorts to school in the warmer weather. This was refused, but later in the year, the principal caved in and we got our wish. Another mention at this meeting was that the school needed the services of a teacher to take cadets. The cadet organisation involved boys volunteering for army training one afternoon a week after school. It also involved an annual camp at an army establishment such as Singleton. These days, girls are also accepted into the Cadet Corps.

After consultation with my wife, I applied for the job, giving as my experience my five years as a cadet myself at school and my recent experience as a national serviceman in the Australian Army. I was immediately signed up; the papers were sent to the appropriate authority, and I was asked to attend the headquarters of the cadet establishment to receive my uniform. Because I had not attended the introductory training school, I was appointed as a Second Lieutenant. I attended a school for new cadet officers in the next school vacation and could then put up a second pip as a full lieutenant.

The cadet unit came with one cadet underofficer, a quartermaster sergeant, and other NCOs and even a small band. I am quite sure that Bill, the Q-sergeant, would have fitted into the job in the permanent army quite well. He knew all the tricks. At the end of the annual camp when we were handing equipment back to the army, we were short of hats. Lots of the kids had lost theirs. Bill overcame that. He handed in the hats we had and deftly retrieved one bunch of hats (neatly tied up in bundles of ten) and handed that in again. No problem. All square. He also made a good scavenger, like all good Q-sergeants.

Enough of cadets for now. I quickly settled in to the new school. Like one of my previous schools, the campus consisted of two sets of buildings. These were separated by a path which took some ten minutes or so to walk. When the principal wanted to travel between the two campuses, he drove. I was situated in the upper school, Years 10–12, while the lower campus consisted of Years 7–9.

All classes from Year 10 were separated into two streams, which no one told me about until, having taken my first class, I was detailed to call a roll. I went through the letters of the alphabet until I came to "M," when the first person owned up. I asked how was it that no one had owned up till then. "We are all M–Z." No one had bothered to mention that to me (or was it just the class taking a rise out of the new teacher?).

Most students were keen to learn, so it was easy to teach them. In recent years, this school became a selective school, taking only the brighter students.

This was the second school I had taught in which had a PA system. There would be a warning buzzer five minutes before the end of a period, then a sound much like the sound when a submarine captain shouts "Dive, Dive!" at the end of the period, and another buzzer five minutes after the end of the period. There was to be no movement after that; everyone was supposed to be in their classroom, ready to start the next lesson. The PA was also selective, so that if Student X was required, the deputy principal who controlled the PA system would look up X's timetable to find out where he or she should be and simply speak to that room. This was unlike the PA in my first school, where the message went out to all classes, who had to "down tools" to listen. I had to use it once before school, when the deputy was not there. I called for the deputy to attend his office to answer the phone. I gave out what I thought was his hyphenated name but which was, in fact, his first and second names. He asked why I had given out his first name to the whole school (some teachers are sensitive about any student knowing their first name). As for me, I never worried.

At this school, all my classes were Science classes. I taught Year 10 only. The older, entrenched staff taught Years 11 and 12. Laboratories were in short supply so one had to plan carefully to ensure that when one was in a laboratory that one could do experiments.

Students had one class a week designated for scripture. This period was given over to visiting clergy or catechists to take a class of their religion. I was allocated a class and had to attend each week because no person came to take the class, and I certainly wasn't going to teach scripture. I noticed in the newspaper that some parents are attempting to remove scripture from the school curriculum. The history of scripture being taught in public schools goes back to the days when all the schools were run by religious organisations. When the state took over education for everyone, the concession was that one period a week was devoted to scripture.

One way of extracting chlorophyll from plants is to boil the leaves in methylated spirit. One day, as I was walking past one of the laboratories, I became aware of a strong smell of methylated spirits. I had only just become aware of this when the Science master came rushing down the corridor to enter the room. His first act was to open the cupboard under the front desk and turn off the gas main. His second act was to order a couple of students to open as many windows as they could, and his third was to speak to the teacher. The teacher was a student from Teachers College. He had the class heating leaves in methylated spirit in beakers over Bunsen burners. If the concentration of methylated spirits vapour had built up just a little more, a Bunsen burner could have exploded, with drastic consequences. What the student should have done was to use electric hot plates, which were available.

Two very notable events occurred to me that year. One was the birth of our first child, the second being the first moon landing. Coincidentally, they occurred at the same time. Our daughter was born as the rocket to the moon took off; the second was witnessed by the world. On the day of the landing, lots of preparations were made. Some students brought radios to school; any TV's owned by the school were transported to rooms (there were very few TV's). The Science Department owned one, which was set up in the front of one of the laboratories.

As the time approached, lessons became increasingly abandoned, students and teachers grouping themselves in places where they could witness the historic events which were about to occur. The principal propped himself squarely in front of the TV in the Science laboratory. The deputy principal became upset because no was moving from one room to another each time the period bell rang. Witnessing this event, the making of history, was far more important. We witnessed the first steps and the historic "One small step for a man, one giant leap for mankind." We stayed on for the subsequent action until the principal declared that school was over for the day and everyone could go home. I went to see my wife and child in hospital. My wife had missed the whole thing. She was otherwise occupied.

Arrangements were made for the annual cadet camp; all units in the area would go into camp together. We travelled by train to the camp and were sent into the countryside around Singleton. Here we set up as one company (none of the schools had very many cadets). Accommodation was provided in the form of six-man tents. The officers of cadets (me included) shared the one tent. We had stretchers for beds. We provided our own sleeping bags.

Cadets, probably no more than the average schoolboy, were reluctant to shower, so we had to have compulsory showers every few days. The cadets had to report on parade in greatcoats and boots with soap and towel, wearing nothing under the greatcoat. The schools had provided special, homemade devices for delivering hot water. They worked on the principle that for every litre of hot water you wanted for the shower, you had to pour the same amount of cold water in. A roaring fire under the equipment provided the heat. So there we were, one Sunday morning, with a line of semi-naked cadets waiting to be showered, when the general in charge of the cadet corps appeared. This did not faze him, and he complimented the unit for its action. He was, in fact, the same general who had inspected the cadets at Mudgee High several years ago. I recognised one of the permanent army officers attached to the camp as the lieutenant in charge of my platoon when I did my National Service. He now had the rank of major.

Cadet units were scheduled to have one day on the rifle range. All cadets who had been in the unit more than one year attended. We were issued with Lee Enfield 0.303 rifles and were bussed to the city rifle range. All went well. At the end of the day, when scores were added up, I had come second. This was even though I had to have a cadet indicate for me exactly where my shots were falling on the target. I just couldn't see the tiny spotting disk.

After we had returned to the school and checked our equipment, one rifle was found to be missing. A phone call to the bus company revealed that we had left one rifle on the bus. A quick trip to the bus company, and I had secured the rifle. These were working weapons; the rifles permanently issued to the school were not suitable for firing. They were really only for drill and instruction.

The principal was a hands-on kind of person. The staff were quite bemused to find one morning that the principal was dressed in old shorts with a ladder and painting equipment, painting a classroom. On occasions, he would think that something needed to be done and just do it.

In June, underground student newspapers began to appear. They had been printed elsewhere. In one issue, the Latin motto of the school was criticised. The principal's reply to this attack was to change the motto. He was a Latin scholar and claimed that the new one was more appropriate than the old one. The newspapers died a swift death, and we heard no more from them.

My sports allocation was to take a team for Australian rules football. Having been brought up on rugby league, I had no idea of the rules and had quickly to learn. Even after many years, although I like to watch a good game of Australian Rules, I still don't know all the regulations.

At the end of the school year, students in their final year held a muck-up day. Many schools did this. Today, the affair seems to have died out. Students met some weeks before the final day and planned it. Usually there were balloons, streamers, and signs (some not all that nice), and the students might attend in old clothes or fancy dress, parading around the school and generally tending to disrupt the classes. This year, the principal met the students, discussed their plans, and gave them funds to buy things. The day went very well.

I went for inspection once again this year and finally got the promotion I was after. At the end of the year, I received notification that I would become Science master in Condell Park High, the position being permanent.

In the school holidays following, I attended a camp for officers of cadets. I had to leave my new daughter with my wife for a week to attend the camp.

I counted this year as being very successful: new daughter, promotion, cadets, a great learning experience. I looked forward to the next year.

11

Permanent at Last

When I rang the principal of my new school to tell him that I was the new acting special master (non-graduate) in charge of Science, he said that he already had one (the term "Acting" meant that I had passed inspection; I could drop the term "Acting" as soon as List 2 had been published).

The person who had been filling in as Science master was known to me. I would be forcing him out of the job. Fortunately, he acquired another relieving job at Engadine High. I took time off from work to go to the new school to meet the principal.

This school did not have a cadet unit, but nearby Bass High did. I contacted the school and the local army establishment and was told that I could assist the teacher who was the officer in charge. I went to camp with this unit.

Once again, I was allocated to take Australian rules football for sport, even though I didn't know all the rules.

One morning before classes began, a car driver decided that he would become a pest, driving round and round the block and driving past the school at high speed. Because this behaviour was endangering our kids, I rang the police. They attended, but the pest had decided that he'd find some other place to amuse himself. The police, finding nothing better to do, carried out inspections of the students' cars which were parked outside the school. They found quite a few infractions such as bald tyres and so on. The students concluded that I had invited the police to inspect their cars. I was not very popular after that.

A new program was introduced by the DET, namely "Learning to

Drive." A local car dealer provided a car, which was garaged at the school, and students who were old enough could learn to drive the car. I took one student. The car had been equipped with additional clutch and brake pedals on the passenger's side of the car. These overrode the normal brake and clutch pedals. I'm afraid that I was too fond of the additional pedals.

One of my Science staff, a woman of short stature, was very fond of short skirts. One day, I passed the room where she was teaching and glanced into the glass panel in the door. I noticed that the front row of boys was crouched down, looking intently up at the teacher. Yes, there she was, reaching up to write on the upper reaches of the board. I glared at the boys and eventually caught their attention, at which they straightened up shamefacedly.

I don't know how this began, but one of the rats we kept for experimental purposes escaped. Immediately, some of the boys in my class undertook the task of capturing it. They pulled out empty drawers and tried to trap the rat under an upturned drawer. Eventually, one of them did, and then the task was to catch the rat and return it to its cage. In the process, a student hit his head and went, with head bleeding, to the office for some first aid. A second student suffered a similar fate after being bitten by the rat, and soon I received a query from the office, asking "what the heck" I was doing. Eventually, the rat was secured and re-caged.

One favourite experiment was Ohm's law, which basically asked, "What is the connection between the current flowing in a circuit and the potential difference across that circuit?" In this school, there were ten benches in each laboratory. To set up this experiment required the following apparatus:

Ten each transformers, rheostats, press switches, voltmeters, ammeters, and resistors, and seventy connecting leads. The seventy leads had me worried so much that I invented "Ohm's law boards." The school had lots of old laboratory stools, which were due to be collected and retired. They were of no further use, so I removed the seat part of ten of them and wired them up with leads and plugs so that students had only to plug in the appropriate equipment in the labelled spaces for the experiment to be set up. This not only saved a lot of trouble and time, it meant that the circuits were set up correctly and saved the lab attendant a lot of trouble.

This went well until I caught two naughty students who should have known better, who were busy removing the labels from the boards. I imposed a fine, a sum which would compensate for the extra tape I would have to buy, not even taking into account the extra time the lab attendant would have to take to repair the damage.

The students refused to pay, but when it came time for me to sign them out when they were leaving school, I refused to sign their clearance papers until they did (I have a long memory). I demonstrated these boards at a Science teachers meeting and believe they were well received.

On the way to school one morning, I noticed that I needed petrol for the car. I called in to one of the local service stations. In those days, service stations had a paper towel dispenser at about head high, so that after inspecting the oil level in your engine, you could wipe your hands. Having done this, I straightened up, driving my head into the toothed edge of the dispenser. My head bled, as all head wounds do. I asked the attendant inside the service station if I could use his sink. At first, without looking at me, he refused, but after one glance, he couldn't get me to the sink fast enough. On the way to school, I stopped at the casualty department of the local hospital (I noticed that service stations no longer have such dispensers any more).

The Science laboratories shared a preparation room. Alongside the room was a small corridor connecting the labs. There were sliding doors leading to this corridor. They were always hard to close, and one day, I gave the door an almighty shove. In the process, the pelmet over the door fell on my head. More blood, and another visit to hospital. Teaching can be dangerous.

I finally graduated as a Bachelor of Arts. During my time at the school, I managed to study and pass three subjects and finally finish the course I had started some twelve years previously. One of the Physical Education teachers was studying the same courses that I was studying, so we helped each other. Since I became a graduate, I was eligible to become the Science Master, as opposed to being the Special Master (non-graduate) in charge of Science.

Once again, in this school, an affair between two teachers was going on under my nose, without my being aware of it. I just don't think that way.

The playground area was quite large, and we could set up an area which was for girls only. The general area was for both boys and girls, but several girls had requested an area where they could be free of boys. Senior girls and boys had another separate area of their own.

On April 25, Australia celebrates Anzac Day, commemorating the brave soldiers from Australia and New Zealand who lost their lives in the

Gallipoli campaign in World War I. The school held its own commemorative ceremony just prior to Anzac Day, which is a public holiday. One year, I was asked to give the oration in which I emphasised that Anzac Day did not glorify war; in fact, it stressed the opposite. It was part of our country's growing up and meant so much to the soldiers who fought there and the families who lost loved ones.

By the time I arrived at this school, photocopying had gone beyond the wet stage but still required a stencil to be made. Once again, I oversaw the photocopier.

The school had acquired a TV recorder using half-inch tape. We taped several programs for the Science Department.

I was still marking Higher School Certificate examinations at the end of the year. This school was much farther away from the marking centre than the previous one, and it required some tricky driving to get to the centre on time.

Once a year, the school had an open night. Students demonstrated experiments to visitors. One of the Science staff demonstrated the thermite reaction. This reaction generated enough heat to melt steel. Unfortunately, the experiment burned quite a hole in the front bench of the laboratory.

Science teachers were hard to get, so the DET decided to import teachers from overseas. At one stage, I had three American teachers on the Science staff. We welcomed them all, guiding them through our methods and the curriculum. One of them, a woman from New York, used to mark the students' workbooks. I happened to note that she had written on one, "What the shit is this?"

I reminded her that while this might be okay in New York schools, it certainly wasn't what we expected here. The same woman remarked to me as we were examining the local invertebrate life on a school field trip that she had noticed an insect with eight legs. I asked her to reconsider that statement and see if she had viewed a spider.

During my time at the school, the DET began funding in-service courses. Science teachers in the region met and decided to set up an area Science Teachers Association. Before long, I became the vice president in charge of in-service courses. We set up many of them which were an immense help to teachers.

One afternoon after school, I had to drive to another school for a meeting. I felt quite woozy and had to rest for several minutes. It was the first symptom I had experienced as part of my diabetes. I didn't know what it was at the time but in later years was told that it was a "hypo."

The biggest event of my time at this school was the addition of our second and third children. We already had one daughter, born after considerable expense trying to find out why we were not able to conceive. We were lucky to have the next two.

I thought that with the extra responsibility of two more children, I should get another work car. I responded to an advertisement and acquired a Hillman Imp, a very small car. It came with a spare engine. The person who sold me the car said that I might have difficulty getting into reverse gear. After one day, I could never get into reverse. This entailed some difficulty in parking. I often parked uphill when I could. Reversing the car was easy: just put it in neutral. The car used to oil up one spark plug so I used to carry a couple of spare spark plugs and would clean up the oiled ones each night. I always knew when the spark plug had been oiled up because the engine would be firing on three cylinders.

Four of the masters in the school requested inspections for List 3. The inspectors came, and two received a favourable result. I did not. However, two years later, I applied again and this time was successful.

One task I had was to train the lab attendant. She was a very good learner and became so good that if I had ordered some equipment for a lesson, she worked out what I had forgotten and supplied that also. She was so good that all orders submitted on time were always there when needed, and five minutes after the lesson, the equipment was washed up and put away.

New courses in Physics and Chemistry were introduced. I taught both to see what snags there might be before rostering other teachers onto those classes.

One day, an acquaintance asked me to fill in for him at evening college. Evening college involves teaching various subjects in public schools after hours. Students could secure qualifications they sought. I taught his class for him at a local school in one of the school laboratories. The lesson proceeded according to plan, but I became a little suspicious that something was not okay. When Science teachers finish the day, they turn off the gas and water mains, which are accessed in a cupboard under the teachers' front desk. Sure enough, when I checked, the water main was turned off, so I turned it on. Every tap in the laboratory gushed water. "Okay, turn them off."

In weeks to come, I secured a permanent job teaching evening college, and later still, I managed to get a job teaching at St George College of Further and Technical Education (TAFE) at night.

My mother died during my time at the school. After providing proof, I was given paid leave to attend to things and the funeral. The school was very kind, and I recall the student captains enquiring after my well-being.

One of my senior classes had twin boys. They were identical and were very hard to tell apart, until one married. Then it was easy: the married one was always smiling. At this school I was thrilled to teach another of the best three Physics students I had ever taught, another girl. Who said that girls couldn't do Physics?

Towards the end of my last year at this school, I was allocated the task of setting the next year's timetable. This was a rather intricate job but was shared with another subject master. It took several hours after school for about a week before we finally finished. The deputy principal was a fan of horse racing. We had to be sure that the timetable gave him Friday afternoons off (DPs taught up to fourteen periods a week, and periods were forty minutes long).

At the end of seven years at this school, I applied for an appointment to a school closer to home. I was appointed to Heathcote High, near where I lived.

12

Close to Home

This appointment was close to home and was very welcome. Initially, I drove to this school by car; in later years, I rode a bicycle to school until, one day, I was forced off the road by a motorist, whence I purchased a motor scooter. No one ran me off the road then.

The Science Department at this school had been overseen by a relieving teacher and was not in good shape. I had to do a lot of reorganising. I produced new policies and guidelines. The two laboratory attendants were pleased that I had acknowledged the part they played in the education of children.

When I inspected the storeroom, I noted that much of the equipment was on the floor, not on the shelves. This annoyed me. The senior of the two laboratory assistants would not allow any teachers to enter her store, but it was okay if I went in. From time to time, I arrived early at school to tidy up and put apparatus in proper places, not on the floor. This was her only foible. She was otherwise very good at her job, as was her assistant.

The lab attendant brought to my intention that we had two large bottles of kerosene, in which sat some quite large lumps of sodium and potassium. These had been "gunking" away for some time, to use the lab assistant's term. I resolved that we would get rid of them. The DET would not take them away, so I came into the school during the school vacation determined to dispose of them.

I am not a maniac, and I do have regard for the environment, but I was desperate. First of all, I tried putting bits into a sink full of water. The action which occurred spat bits of metal in all directions. I then decided that I would dispose of the sodium and potassium in a nearby dam. When I got there, there were people swimming, so I moved on. I found another creek; some potassium went into the creek, but this caused so much smoke (and it was in a bushfire season) that I decided, "Not there." I decided to try the ocean. I drove to a deserted beach. The first piece of sodium went off with a bang in the surf. People came from everywhere to see what was going on. Back to school.

After suiting myself in my lab coat and motor cycle helmet, I managed to dispose of the offending metals by throwing bits into a large garbage bin, adding water all the time with a hose. As the bin overflowed, the overflow went into a drain. I know that the above was not environmentally sound, but what was I to do? The DET would not handle the stuff. There were many other bottles of chemicals which could be dangerous. In fact, one bottle's label declared that the bottle should not be shaken in case it exploded. Why these chemicals were there, nobody knew. The University of New South Wales came to our aid in taking some of them including some fifty bottles of xylol away.

Because of my experience in my previous school in regard to in-service of teachers, I revived the local Science Teachers Association and became the officer in charge of organising in-service courses. This went well, and I organised many courses. Within some twelve months, an inspector decided that things were going so well that he took over the job. I have to say that things did not go as well after he took over.

The Science staffroom in this school was very tiny. Six teachers were crammed into an office designed for two. As well as us, there were two big filing cabinets. It was nearly at the point where teachers had to breathe in to allow others to pass behind them. I prevailed on the principal, and he had the room expanded into an adjacent classroom; workmen took down one wall and erected another farther away. This at least gave us some breathing space.

One day, in this new setup, one of my teachers told me that the intercom phone rang incessantly. He was trying to do some work in his "free" period but was constantly interrupted. In the end, he told me, when the phone rang again, he picked it up and threw it into the garbage bin. He said that not more than one minute had elapsed when the principal burst through the door, complaining about his call being cast into the garbage.

We had a teacher whose desk was piled so high that he could no longer lay his hands on his textbooks. His solution was to take the desired textbook from a nearby desk. This situation led to teachers identifying their textbooks prominently with their names. If they later found their textbook had disappeared, they knew where to find it.

We also had another teacher who wanted to ignore the program as set and teach his own material. This and other problems, such as the teacher who objected to a smoker in the room (in the days when it was legal to smoke in staffrooms), demanded appropriate intervention on my behalf. I learned a lot about staff management.

The Science laboratories were in two buildings some hundred metres apart. There were two in "B" block and two in "D" block. I chose to take my practical lessons in D block. Here I stored all the teaching aids I had accumulated over the years; I even put up some of the posters in the window facing the student corridor.

This part of Sydney is notable in having a high population of funnel-web spiders. The funnel-web spider is one of the most venomous spiders in the world. It is very aggressive. Its fangs can even penetrate toenails, so if you are going to step on one, make sure that you are wearing shoes. These nasty things could kill a small child and make older people very sick. Fortunately, antivenoms were developed to counteract the spider's poisonous bite. The antivenom is available to hospitals. The area in which I live is one of their favourite habitats. The spiders are called funnel-webs because the entrance to their burrow in the ground has a spider web funnel. They catch their food, usually insects, by sneaking up on them and then pouncing.

Aware that there were so many spiders in the area, one university sent its people to catch the spiders, which were then killed and encased in plastic blocks, which were then distributed to schools.

One teacher asked a student to go outside into the bush at the back of the school to collect some leaf litter. The class he was teaching was studying the animals which live in leaf litter. When the student came back, the teacher saw a funnel web in the leaf litter. He told the student to put the litter on the floor gently. He then found the spider and stepped on it.

The possum is an Australian native. In many ways, it's the squirrel of Australia, although they are not related. What I mean is that they are just as annoying. We live close to Royal National Park. The school mentioned is about 150 yards from where I live now. Possums often get in under roofs and set up their living quarters, including their lavatories. Consequently, people find that mysterious smell and wonder what it is until someone says, "You've got possums." Park rangers will come and collect the offending possums, but they don't clean up the mess. Possums have murderous claws, so we keep shy of touching them. I was driving to the shops just a few days ago, and a mother possum with a youngster clinging to her back ran across the road right in front of me.

One morning, we arrived at school to find a possum sitting in a gas cupboard. Gas cupboards were used to contain experiments which would produce dangerous and poisonous fumes. They had a flue which went out through the roof. The possum had found his way into the flue and fell into the cupboard. A teacher wearing protective clothing (because of the claws) rescued the possum and returned him to the bush. When we found the possum in the cupboard again, we asked the DET to cover the top of the flue with a mesh.

Canteens in schools are often known as tuckshops. It just so happened that the lady who ran the tuckshop in that school was named Mrs Tuck. She previously had a canteen in a primary school. When she moved her business to the high school, the kids in the primary school thought that that was the end of their tuckshop. Tuckshops sold such things as hot pies, sausage rolls, potato crisps, all sorts of candy, soft drinks, and so on; in other words, treats for the kids and things that were not really healthy. In recent years, the DET has banned the sale of many items so that only healthy food can be sold.

The principal held his executive meetings on sports afternoons. All subject heads attended. Mail specific to departments was distributed, and plans for the weeks ahead were discussed. The rest of the staff took various sporting teams. I found the meetings rather boring and had to fight to stay awake. I solved that problem by volunteering to take minutes.

Like many schools, dances were held in the school hall at night. The first time I attended one of these dances, we found that one boy had become drunk and was found on the roof of the hall. We managed to get him down, and a teacher drove him home to his parents. The next day, his father complained that the school was supplying students with liquor.

During the time when the school had a permanent Science master, many Blue Messels had been purchased. His idea was to introduce programmed learning. The students answered questions on paper after referring to the books. He had also wired up the desks in one laboratory so that students could press a button to answer yes or no to a question. Then, after asking a question, he could see from the monitor he had set up who had answered yes and who had answered no. I dismantled this and decided that our program would not need this setup.

The school was fortunate to have a good drama teacher, and very entertaining plays were presented in the school hall. Parents and neighbours attended the plays in large numbers. The attendance ticket sales helped the school budget.

The school had two football fields. I staged a star night, in which I provided two telescopes and pointed out several of the prominent stars and constellations. In later years, after I left the school, several of the students who had attended the night told me they never forgot it.

I also used this field, which fortunately ran north-south, for a demonstration in which a long wire was moved at right angles to the earth's magnetic field. A minute current was registered on a micro-ammeter. Two students held the wire which extended across the field and, on a cue moved the wire quickly up and don.

Each year, the school sent its Year 11 students to camp, which was staffed by state school teachers. Several schools did the same. The students and teachers were accommodated in rooms which once housed the workers on the Snowy Mountains scheme many years before. The students were put into groups consisting of students from several different schools, so that they had to mix. These groups stayed together for the duration of the camp. Each day, they were passed from one member of the permanent staff to another to learn some lessons in bushcraft and social skills. In recent years, this camp has been discontinued. It did a good job and kept teachers on their toes, especially at night, when panty raids and other meetings were discouraged. Valuable lessons were learned here including improvement of the students' social skills.

One year, I was one of the teachers who accompanied the students to the camp. We travelled by train and bus. Each night, all the students were to attend functions in the camp hall (compulsory fun). On the last night, our teachers went around checking all the rooms to ensure that all students were attending the dance which had been put on. In one room, I came across an acrid smell and wondered what it was. Yes, it was marijuana, and the student whose room it was had to report to the principal after his return to school. The student subsequently left the school before he was expelled.

One of my beginning teachers had been arrested for taking drugs. The DET moved quickly, suspending the teacher and subsequently firing him. I recall the teacher pleading with me for a refence, which I could not give under the circumstances. I always hoped that his life went well after that incident because, despite his failing, he seemed to be a good teacher.

Another teacher was found to be a child molester. The response of the DET was to move him to another school. This was typical of things in those days, when authorities really didn't know what to do: "just move them on" after some ineffectual counselling.

One experiment in the senior Chemistry syllabus involved preparing methane gas. I found a reputable textbook which showed how to produce the gas. The teacher whose class was doing senior Chemistry went ahead with a demonstration, using the recipe from the book. Unfortunately, the experiment blew up. One girl in the class suffered slight damage to her eye. Her father rightly called for an investigation to be performed. An inspector came out and did a thorough job, finding that nothing wrong had been done. The textbook, as I said, was reputable. It was a pure accident, with no apparent cause. The teacher was declared to not be at fault. We never did that experiment again.

An acquaintance of mine, another Science teacher, was setting up a book publishing firm. He invited me to join a small group who were writing questions for a book to be published on senior Biology. Thus began my writing career. I received due recognition, and my name appeared on the author's page. A thought came to me, and I decided to write a similar book for Physics. I did this and submitted the finished work to the publisher. I heard nothing for a time, but then the publisher told me that he had not gone ahead with the book; he gave me $1,000 for my work. Good.

A few weeks later, a girl came into my class one day and showed me a book she had bought: my book. I received a minor credit, the publisher claiming the major credit for himself. This did not sit well with me, and I decided that I would go freelance. I spoke with a bookseller, who was a regular visitor to the school. He said that if I came up with the goods, he would get them published. I did, and he did, so I became a published author in my own right. Fortunately, I kept the copyright. I revised this book several times, as new syllabuses were introduced.

A funny thing happened to me at TAFE. On the first night I was to teach a class, I was talking to the lab attendant when a teacher put his head around the door from his classroom, asking the attendant to make twenty copies of a certain page in a certain book. I immediately recognised the book as being one of my own (I had written another book by then). I asked the lab attendant how the author would feel if he knew that someone was blatantly copying his work. She replied that he would never know.

I said that she was looking at the author. I believe she nearly had a stroke, apologising profusely. I said that all was okay. I met her years after, and she said she had not forgotten that incident. Later again, another acquaintance was writing an academic paper on copyright. He asked my permission to use the above story. Of course, I gave him permission, and with a couple of changes to the story, it became part of his paper.

One favourite trick performed by students in classes was to disconnect the plumbing under the laboratory benches. One day, the teacher instructed the class to light up their Bunsen burners, unaware that the gas line under one bench had been disconnected. The result was that the underside of that bench erupted in flames, and one girl whose underpants caught fire was slightly injured. Science can be dangerous.

Every state school has one period a week set aside for scripture. Ministers and volunteers come into the school and teach their brand of religion. Because not all parents wanted their children to attend scripture and there was a shortage of people to take the classes, the principal scheduled the scripture lesson to be at the end of the day. Students who did not attend scripture could go home, and staff could do the same after the final bell for the day. This was not popular with the ministers and scripture teachers, but the policy prevailed.

I had a policy of temporarily promoting truculent students in low-level classes to a top class I was teaching, where the students would not tolerate the performance of the "promoted" students, who often begged to go back to their original class, where they promised to be good. I did this to one girl, and she complained to the mistress of girls. I was carpeted in the principal's office with the principal and the mistress of girls on the other side of the desk. I had to rescind the move. Some years later, the same girl was in a lot of trouble. I reminded the principal that if I had my way years ago, this might not have happened.

The English master was always boasting that he had the biggest department in the school. One year, when new courses had been introduced, I counted the number of periods taught in his and my departments. The result was that Science had one more period than English. At the next executive meeting, I casually mentioned that Science was the biggest department. This really shocked the English master.

Can you imagine a painter who just painted over everything? On one memorable occasion, painters descended on the school. I was glad that no children stood for any length of time near the painter. I suspect that he would have painted them. He painted everything, including a trail of ants under the roof of a covered walkway. Normally, people would have brushed the ants out of the way, but not this painter. From that time, the fossilized ants could still be seen trapped in the paint.

When I first started at the school, I received a promotion at the Higher School Certificate marking centre. I became a senior assistant examiner, which meant that I was in charge of ten people who marked higher school certificate biology papers. I held this position for many years until the authorities wanted to try new people. Altogether I had been marking for twenty-five years. Each afternoon after school, we would make a dash for the cars and drive to the Sydney showground. There were several markers of various subjects at this school.

Each week, the school held a full assembly. The assemblies were chaired by one of the subject masters or mistresses. The principal and deputy principal also spoke at the assemblies. On one memorable occasion, the deputy complained about the boys who played at recess and lunchtime in an area of the playground below his window. He exhorted the boys to stop bashing their balls against his wall. In case this escapes some readers, some listeners interpreted this as meaning "stop banging your testicles against the wall." This remark resulted in howls of laughter from the assembly. The deputy retired in embarrassment. He had, in fact been complaining about the game students were playing in the playground which adjoined his study. The game involved hitting a tennis ball against the wall in a game similar to squash.

One day when I was running this assembly, I got into a little trouble when I dismissed the school with the order to "break off." This order was in common usage in the army, meaning to dismiss, and it came to me naturally. I had accidently used it. The principal thought that I had ordered "rack off," a rather rude expression meaning "fuck off." I quickly explained the incident to him but was never sure that he accepted my explanation.

After some three years at the school, I was afflicted by a problem with my knee. It was very painful and was diagnosed as a cartilage problem. My doctor recommended a surgeon, and he operated to snip off the offending bit of cartilage. After the operation, I had to take time in recovery, which took a couple of weeks. I could hardly walk. I was on crutches before and after the operation. Fortunately for me, I was rarely sick enough to have to take sick leave. When it came time for me to retire, I had accumulated one year's sick leave, which expired as I retired.

Teachers union meetings were held each month. At one meeting, the union representative spent much energy exhorting us to join in the forthcoming strike, which had been organised by the state union. He said that we must strike. At the end of the meeting, I retorted, "*Sieg Heil*," and raised my arm in a Nazi salute. I have never believed that teachers should go on strike. The principal later said jokingly to me that I had never saluted him.

In my last year at the school, when a new building was being built, a portable demountable Science laboratory was delivered to the school. I scheduled all my practical periods to be held in this building. One day, I came in to find that a front-end loader machine was busy digging a trench along one side of the building. It was pretty noisy. This wasn't the end of the story, however. A worker started cutting concrete on the other side of the building. When the first class came in, I wrote on the board:

GOOD MORNING.

COLLECT YOUR TEXTBOOKS FROM THE FRONT OF THE ROOM AND TURN TO PAGE …

ANSWER THE QUESTIONS IN YOUR WORKBOOK.

SORRY ABOUT THE NOISE.

While I had a class in this laboratory, I finally caught a student whose favourite trick was to dismantle a gas tap during a lesson. The gas taps at that time were very vulnerable to being taken apart and then reassembled in such a way that they looked to be okay but would leak as soon as the gas main, operated by the teacher, was turned on. Students doing this were hard to catch. Normally, the gas main in each laboratory would be turned off except when in use. In my laboratory, I kept the main in the on position during the lesson, turning it off as I left the laboratory. As soon as the trickster had dismantled the gas tap, the resulting "hiss" of escaping gas betrayed his trick to everyone, and he was in trouble.

It was about this time when new gas heaters were installed in the school. Each had a piezo-electric ignition switch to light the gas. It took one week for enterprising students to strip every ignition switch from every new gas heater. I found out later that students believed that they could use the switch to operate fun parlour machines, avoiding having to pay to use them. I don't know if this was true. All I know is that we had to light the gas with a match from there on. I wondered if we would ever win the war against destruction.

In my last year, the school was introduced to computers. There were several models on the market, many using tapes to store information. We examined several types and finally settled on the Apple Computer 2E. I became very interested in this and began to improve my skills. I even attended a course on how to use it. At first, I learned to play some games. This led to more academic usage. I determined that I would encourage the use of computers at my next school.

This school produced some really talented students. A girl in one of my Physics classes (the last of the three top students I had taught) later became a professor of Physics at a university. Another student studied medicine at university and has now become a well-recognised medical specialist. One talented student left school after completing his School Certificate at the end of Year 10 to become an apprentice motor mechanic. Some teachers bemoaned this as "a waste of his talent." I asked them, who they would like to work on their motor car: him or another student who had barely scraped through the School Certificate and had also become an apprentice motor mechanic.

Booksellers came regularly to the school, touting their range of textbooks. I spoke to one about the books I had written and said I would like to write another. I wanted to write a book of senior Physics questions. He said that he would publish the book, which he did. After the initial run of the book, he sold it to another publishing firm This firm went through two revisions until finally withdrawing the book from publication. After some years, I managed to find another publisher, who took the book and published it. It has since gone through several revisions and is still being sold. I retain the copyright and receive a small royalty.

After nine years at the school, the longest time I had spent at any school, I finally achieved my ambition to become a deputy principal and moved on.

I enjoyed my time at this school. I thought that I was ready to take on the role of Deputy Principal. Since my retirement and move to a retirement village, I now live close to this school and often come into contact with some of my students, who are glad to see me and chat with me. I don't remember the faces, but when I ask their name, memories come back. In the case of women, I have to ask, "Who were you?" as, in most cases, they have changed their name having married.

13

Big Time

I received a letter from the DET promoting me to the position of Deputy Principal of Miller High. That afternoon, I drove to the school to have a look. While walking around, I came to the attention of one of the cleaners. I explained who I was and why I was there. When I rang the Principal next day, he said that he was aware of my visit (spies everywhere).

This was a co-ed school in a very deprived part of the city. Years ago, the state government had moved many people from city slums to a new area. They built housing and provided facilities, including schools, but there was no work, no transport, and very few shops. This part of the suburbs was often referred at as "Dodge City," because many residents tried very hard to dodge paying bills. Many residents were on government welfare.

The students at the school came from some forty-three different countries. There was a sizeable number of Lebanese migrants. The school also had an Intensive Learning Unit, housing several Vietnamese students who had to be exposed to education and also learn English.

I quickly settled into the job, asking the Principal for two things: a telephone that could store twenty phone numbers of casual teachers I could ring when needed and a computer. I quickly found out that I was lucky to have one casual I could ring, occasionally two, but I still got the phone. After making enquiries, I found that the school had one computer, which resided in the Mathematics Department storeroom and was used by no one.

It took me several months for the Principal to agree to my second request, which was to acquire an Apple 2E computer. I bought the computer (black and white monitor), a printer, a stand for the printer, and rolls of paper for the printer. I set it up in the ante room to my office and set about encouraging teachers to come and play games on it. This is good training. At the same time, I bought a program I could use to set up class lists. Class lists were a problem due to the practice of some Vietnamese students, who used different ones of their customary three names to acquire extra benefits, such as being able to borrow three times as many books from the school's library as anyone else. I produced the lists, distributed them, and gradually won the confidence of the Principal, who could not contain his excitement, and then the staff, who could see what the computer could do.

The school also had a Behaviourally Disturbed unit, which had six students taught by one teacher. This unit operated largely independently of the rest of the school. The school also had a printing unit from the Disadvantaged Schools Program, which was also completely independent of the school.

The Principal was a likeable man, several years my senior, who I never really got to know. He would start a conversation and, thinking of something else he had to attend to, literally run out of the room and leave me suspended. He wanted us to have lunch together, but it never eventuated. He had his own filing system: on top of his desk. There were piles of files and papers, but he knew where every document was and could instantly find one when needed. After one term, he retired, and another principal was appointed. He had great ideas, and if he had survived as principal, the school would have developed differently. More of this later.

On my first day as deputy, I toured the playground at lunchtime. I came across students shooting balls at the basketball ring. I picked up a ball and shot, scoring a goal. I walked into the Industrial Arts staffroom and, espying a dart board, threw a dart, which lodged in the 50! I have never had any such luck again.

As in previous schools, dances were held. The school did not have a hall. Instead, a rather large open-air gymnasium was used. We had our share, unfortunately, of students arriving at the dance drunk. It was a constant problem in the district. Children would come from dysfunctional families who were alcoholics, and they, in turn, became alcoholics. Several students in this school apparently came from homes where the parents were often drunk. The students would then raid their parents' cellar and drink to oblivion. They sometimes came to school with a cask of wine. This could not be tolerated at a school dance, so the offender had to be escorted home. On one occasion, I had to guard one student who was blind drunk to keep him away from other students. His parents were called to the school to collect their child, but they took their time to arrive. A band called the Cockroaches was playing in the school gymnasium, and our drunk was trying to join the audience. Some who read this might remember that most of the Cockroaches became the Wiggles.

The school had a very good library. It managed to keep its books secure by having strong bars on the windows and a strongroom door fitted as its front door. During one renovation of the school, the builders were puzzled as to why the school insisted that the door had to be so strong. Had it not been, we would have lost all the books.

Vandalism was rife. A favourite stunt was to remove the flagpole and dump it into the nearby creek. It was usually found and was restored. On one occasion, the principal ordered a new one and had it installed. When they found the old one, he had it cut to pieces and disposed of. The flagpole rope was cut so many times that marine cable was fitted, foiling any attempts to cut that.

The principal used a grant to buy and plant a hundred trees around the school. Students were involved in the planting and care of the seedlings. One night two weeks later, every one of the new plants was uprooted and thrown around.

School funds were used to buy twenty keyboards for the Music Department. One night, the room was broken into, and the keyboards were stolen. The thieves didn't want the keyboards; they just wanted to ensure that others couldn't have them. They were found, smashed, in the local creek. Bars for the windows and a security door were ordered for the Music room.

One year, two days before the Christmas vacation was to end, I was telephoned by the DET to go to the school, where 110 windows had been smashed. There was glass and sheets of copy paper everywhere. I informed the local inspector that it was unlikely school would commence on the prescribed day. He contacted glaziers and cleaners, and every window was repaired and the school tidied up by the next day.

Graffiti was a perennial problem. Sometimes, it attacked the school. Other times, it had nothing to do with the school, as at the time when the graffiti "artist" referred to someone who had stolen his girlfriend. It was a costly business just to keep up with getting graffiti removed. It became so bad that the DET contracted to pay for the removal if the cost exceeded $500. The repairs people would sometimes give two quotes for removal of graffiti, depending on who was to pay for it. We had to take the cheaper quote.

Like all state and private schools in Australia, the school had a uniform. A good 20 percent of the students did not wear it or wore only part of it. Boys liked to wear flannel shirts completely unbuttoned over the school shirt, and girls wanted to wear anything black over everything. I ran school assemblies. One day, I mounted the rostrum wearing a flannel shirt over my shirt. It seemed to have the desired effect, as students could see how ridiculous it looked. Flannel shirts disappeared not long after this.

Absenteeism was a huge problem. 20 percent of the students would be absent on a typical day. This rarely worried many parents, who wanted the kids to be at home to run messages or do shopping. Preparing absentee lists to be distributed to all classes was a problem, until I devised a system where the computer printed the names of all absentees from the roll-call slips, which had to be returned after roll-call first thing each morning.

The toilets did not have toilet paper available. Whenever the cleaners put a new roll in the toilet, someone would ram the roll into the toilet basin and then urinate on it (or worse). Consequently, toilet paper was kept at the office, available to students on request.

In my first year, I was contacted by the Red Cross to see if we would sell badges on their appeal day. I said that we would and set about organising students to sell the badges. We did quite well, until one student "lost" the money on the day sit was collected. The same student ultimately could not be relied on for anything, despite his loving parents, who continually tried to bribe him into better behaviour.

I called a parent in one day for an interview about his son's behaviour. The child had put his fist through a glass window in a classroom door. At the end of the interview, I asked the father who was going to pay for that. His response was that the DET had insurance policies to cover that sort of thing.

Some students would do anything to get into a fight. We had twin boys who, when they were not fighting each other, would pick a fight with someone else. Their poor father had to be invited to the school several times to take his suspended offspring home. One favourite trick the bullies used was to tell a student that another student had said something about his mother. Invariably, the bullied student would be Muslim and would believe that he had to defend his mother. Another fight would erupt, and the bully could sit and watch the entertainment.

On one occasion, a very excitable girl had to be escorted off the playground. She had been upsetting others with her bullying and had assaulted some other girls. As she was being led back to the office, one of her victims walked behind her. Quick as a flash, the bully backhanded the victim, breaking her nose.

I was always on the lookout for ex-students and out-of-work young people who thought they could wander into the school at recess and lunchtime when they felt like it. Sometimes, they were looking to start a fight with one of the students. When I ordered one such person to leave our school, he spat in my face. I stared him down, and he eventually retreated.

In many ways, this school was a battlefield; it would have been treated that way, except for the fact that the teachers knew the whole community was hurting. It needed help, and the school was going to give it. The school acted more as a welfare agency than an educational facility. The school operated many programs as a disadvantaged school and provided opportunities for talented students to reach their full potential. Dedicated teachers would not give up and continued to support students to the best of their ability. Some teachers found the school to be too hard for them and requested transfers. I can't say I blame them, but others who were on the staff in my time are still at the school, after having been there for over twenty years.

Like most Australians, the students loved their sport, and the school was the only way they could participate. The school had some very talented teachers of sport, and the school did well in interschool competitions. The school had its own football field, and parents were well in attendance at any game.

I could go on detailing many incidents which occurred in my time at the school. They are many, but I felt (and still feel now) that I was needed there, and it was very rewarding. This community was hurting. It needed us, and we gave all that we could. In all my years as a teacher, I have never seen such a dedicated faculty.

After the principal retired at the end of first term, a new principal was appointed. The new principal had grand plans for improvement, but he suffered from a skin complaint, which eventually caused him to take extended periods of sick leave. When he was away, I was the relieving principal. After some two absences of several weeks, he then went on indefinite sick leave. I relieved in this position for two years. Then it was all up to me. I made very few changes but supported the excellent work which was being done by the school's talented teachers.

A new teaching position was introduced in my first year, that of a Leading Teacher. Leading Teachers had the same status as Deputy Principals but were specially selected based on their ability as teachers. They were appointed to schools to help supervise and support teachers. The DET promised that they would be eligible for promotion in a brief time.

During these two years, the school continued its provisions for extra things through the disadvantaged schools program. I changed school rules from negative to positive (e.g., "don't" became "do"); a new discipline program was commenced, one which placed the responsibility for a student's behaviour on the student, with a solution that students could follow to overcome their problems. Support was given to families where student absenteeism was a problem.

A new initiative of the government introduced Technology schools, which were twinned with Technical colleges and were supported by various industries. Most Technology schools were supplied with computers by their sponsor industry. This school missed out, having to buy its own computers, but at a discount. Miller High became Miller Technology High School.

After the principal came to the end of his sick leave, the position had to be advertised, and I applied for it. I was not selected from the interviewees. It went to a woman leading teacher. Leading Teachers had been promised swift promotion to principal positions. I had done nothing wrong, but I was not the type of person the interviewing panel were looking for, so I was passed over. It was a bitter pill, but life goes on.

The new principal started in the new year, and I took some long service leave. I worked as a casual teacher in several Catholic schools until I was given a block of one term's work at All Saints Senior High School, a Catholic school for a time This went well. I returned to the school as Deputy Principal and applied to transfer to several schools. None of the applications was successful, so at the end of the year, I formally resigned from the DET. However, before I did so, I secured a position as an ordinary classroom teacher at a Catholic college. My teaching career was not over.

14

Back to the Ranks

My final permanent position was in St Mary's Cathedral College, a Catholic boys' school in the city. I was hired to teach senior (HSC) Physics, Chemistry, and Mathematics. It had been several years since I had taught Maths at a senior level. I distinctly recall on my first day being asked by a Mathematics student if the "cosine" was an odd or even function. I honestly had no idea but said, "Even." When I looked it up later, I found that my guess had been correct.

I was really at home with the subjects, and it was so great that I was teaching only senior classes. Another bonus was that the school had its own parking lot under the college (independent and Catholic high schools are often called colleges), which was accessed by a special key. This allowed me to park at the school at night or weekends when I wanted to visit attractions in town.

It wasn't long before the curriculum coordinator had me analysing HSC examination results. The headmaster was very keen to have statistics on how each subject had fared in the examinations, and I was to be the one providing the statistics. I thought I did a good job, and the headmaster agreed. The information was also welcomed by the various subject heads.

The school did not have a reward system, and I decided to propose one. Some teachers told me that what I suggested would never work in this school. This made me determined that I would go ahead. I introduced bronze-coloured cards for students who did a good job in class. If they collected five bronze cards in one subject area, they were eligible for a silver card. Three silver cards from different faculties were rewarded with a gold card. This system had been used in my previous school. I made sure that the first opportunity I had, I would award a silver card for achievement in Science. The scheme caught on and was well thought of.

The allocation of students to roll classes had always been decided on an alphabetical basis. At the stage when I joined the staff, there had been an influx of Asian students. Lists were drawn up according to the alphabetic plan. When it came to the class that I would take, there were so many Asian students that everyone in the class had a name starting with the letter "L." It was decided that this was not a good idea, so the system was made random. In my Year 11 Mathematics Level 2 class, there were twenty-three students, twenty-one of whom were Asian, one South American, and one born here, Anglo-Saxon. The class kept me on my toes.

The laboratory attendant had been working at the school for some time, and we got on well together. However, when I wanted special apparatus to be assembled and did it myself, she became quite annoyed. I found that I had to tread warily at times. This came to a head once when I proceeded to make what I called "puzzle leads." Two leads protruded from each end of a heavily wrapped section of wires but there was no way of automatically deciding which of the two leads from either end of the wrapped section were connected. I made up the leads for a practical test.

While I was at the school, a new edition of my book *Tutorial Problems in HSC Physics* was produced. I immediately ordered a class set. This saved me a lot of work writing problems on the board. Because I held the copyright, it was no problem to photocopy several pages for homework.

I had occasion one day to leave a senior class for a few minutes while I attended to a summons by the headmaster (no problem). When I returned, I was confronted by the sight of one student pointing a gun at another. I really thought that the gun was real and left the class once more to grab the First Assistant (deputy headmaster) to attend. As it turned out, the gun was fake, although it appeared very real. The gun was confiscated and the student disciplined.

At a school athletics carnival, as I was patrolling the seating stands, the headmaster asked me to keep the students from moving around, enquiring if they had a good reason for their movement. Not long after this, I stopped one senior student, who promptly abused me for asking. I reported the incident to the headmaster, who asked the student to apologise.

After the carnival, when normal school resumed, I awaited the apology. It didn't come. One morning, the senior coordinator (in charge of Year 12 classes) asked if I wanted to see the student. I said yes. However, the student didn't come, and I didn't receive the apology.

A few days after this incident, the headmaster summoned me and accused me of interfering with his discipline. He also said that I should have reported the incident at the carnival to the senior coordinator. As one who had experience of being a principal, I thought that his action with this particular student was lacking, but I didn't say so. I merely said that I had no intention of interfering and that I had reported the student to him because he had initially given me the instruction. The upshot was that the student did not ever apologise and was suspended for a few days. I really think that the senior coordinator had set me up, for some reason.

In my second year at this school, I was given a class of Level 4 Mathematics. It had been a long time since I had done my BA, and I had forgotten so much. The trouble with Maths is that there is so much. I recalled attending a lecture given by the professor of pure Mathematics as part of my study of Mathematics III. He said that what we had been studying was old hat in 1850. He was going to introduce us to something which was right up to date. He showed us some of the modern material (Topology) and said that this was where the modern research was.

I accepted the challenge of teaching four units and straight away enrolled in two in-service courses for level 3 and level 4 Mathematics teachers. These were very useful and were paid for by the school. The work was challenging, and when the results came out at the end of the year, one of my students had secured a pass in the top 10 percent of the state.

During that year, we had acquired another teacher in the Mathematics Department. Towards the end of the year, the coordinator of Mathematics went on leave, naming me as coordinator of Mathematics. Before he left, he told me what teachers he wanted to teach what next year. As it turned out, he didn't return, which left me with being coordinator of Mathematics, a job I didn't really want.

As head of Mathematics, I was control of the photocopier. Each teacher was given an allocation of so many copies. The teachers were given a code. The code and the number of copies were entered into the photocopier. That became my job. I allocated the codes to the teachers, who could change the code to one of their own. I asked the head of religious studies if she would be happy with the code "666," as you will remember is the "Devil's number" but she declined. If teachers wanted to exceed the allocated number, they were free to argue their case with the headmaster or pay for the extra copies.

The next year, because I had stated that I really wasn't interested in being coordinator of Mathematics (I had been there, done that, and preferred to give the younger teachers a chance). I was persuaded to take on the role of coordinator of senior Mathematics, while another teacher was given the role of coordinator of junior Mathematics. This worked well. At the end of the year, the two roles were amalgamated again, and applications were called for. The role was offered to me, but I was not interested.

I have never been much good at chess but thought that the school could support a chess club. We bought some chess sets and put our names down to compete against other schools. This gave the boys a lot of experience in chess, and although we didn't do very well, they had fun. One afternoon, after playing another school, we drove back to the school (I drove the players to their venues). When I stopped at a pedestrian crossing to allow someone to cross the road, a car ran into the back of mine. My car needed repairs, which were paid for by the other driver's insurance. A few days after this, I started to experience bad headaches, eventually diagnosed as whiplash. It took many visits to the physiotherapist to fix the problem. As it transpired, I had taught the physiotherapist at one of my previous schools.

My sports allocation during the years was to take a group to lawn bowling. There was a bowling club nearby. The club was good, lending bowls to us. I persuaded the school to buy a set of bowls. Because the boys did not have bowling shoes, they had to go onto the greens in stockinged feet.

The first assistant (deputy principal) did all the allocation of teachers to classes, taking advice from the heads of subjects. He allocated me to teach Level 4 Mathematics for another year. I knew that the previous head of Mathematics had wanted the new teacher to teach that class. I couldn't tell the First Assistant that because he would have just dismissed it. Instead, I had to keep insisting that I thought it would be in the best interests of the students if the new teacher taught the class. After all, her knowledge, being not long out of university, was more up to date. After some argument, the First Assistant saw it my way, and I was off the hook. However, from that time on, I was allocated to one junior class of Mathematics (punishment?).

In my last year, one of my classes was computer studies. I have to say that at that stage, the use of computers by students was just in its infancy. I was given the task of devising a program with the assistance of the one teacher in the school who had a good working knowledge of computers. I taught the class for one period a week, but it didn't come to much.

In my last year, I was also given the task of setting up the timetable for the whole school. I had had experience in a previous school. I did my best, but the crunch came when I informed the first assistant that I had finished. From Years 8 to 12, classes were parallel. Year 7 was not. The first assistant wanted Year 7 to be parallel as well, but I could not do it. He brought in an expert, who started again, only to find that he couldn't do it either. I left, not knowing (or caring) what solution he came to.

At lunch, the staff retired to the common room, which was well furnished. The same groups of people met at the same tables each day. Although I finished at that school some twenty years ago (as I write this), I still keep in contact with them.

At awards day in my final year, one of the students from my senior Mathematics class gave me a greeting card which said, "You taught me to think." I thought that that was I had been trying to do for all the years I had been teaching, and someone had finally said it. What a way to finish a career.

15

Casual

I spent twelve years as a casual or substitute teacher: contacting schools to tell them that I was available, listening for the telephone early in the morning, eat breakfast, pack lunch, drive to the school, get the schedule, and contact the head teacher.

This was a new deal altogether. I was available to both state and Catholic schools. I preferred Catholic schools, for the very good reason that they gave me a detailed explanation of what to teach each class in the day, and they were not afraid to offer a block. The teacher who was absent for the day had to give detailed instructions for the casual who took his or her place.

State schools did not give me a detailed explanation of what to teach each class in the day. What usually happened was that the subject head teacher would describe the work to be covered. This was okay, but what often happened was that the class would say, whether this was true or not, that "we did this yesterday," in which case I was stuck. If the class was in my subject areas, Maths or Science, I could overcome this, but in other subject areas, I did not have the competence to teach something, in which case the class would have to review their work or catch up on other lessons. Occasionally, I could do something. I recall teaching a Year 11 class about family law. It must have gone over well because at the end of the lesson, one student asked if I was a teacher of Legal Studies.

After a brief time, I was contacted by regulars. I worked so often at one school, I was invited to line up with the staff for the staff photo. Being there so often meant that I grew familiar with the layout of the school building and became familiar to students. Casuals can have a pretty torrid time until students realise that they really know what they're talking about. I recently met a woman who had been taught by me when I was a casual at her school, and she complimented me as being someone who "really knew his stuff."

An advantage of being a casual is that if you don't like the school, its ambience, or the students generally, you can always reject any calls they make, until they get tired of trying to get you. Some schools have so many casuals on their books that they cannot employ all of them, but I taught in one school where I was lucky to be on their list.

After I had become a favourite at a couple of schools, I bought a mug, tea, and coffee, which I was able to store at each of the schools. There is nothing worse than bludging off the supplies the permanent staff had paid for.

I began to collect worksheets in various subjects. I could get them copied by the school and kept them handy in case they were needed. One thing I really detested was to be presented with a series of overhead projectuals I had to present to the class so that they could copy the work into their workbooks. In many cases, I asked the office to make copies of the material and issued these to the class; after allowing them to paste the work into their books, we would discuss what they had pasted.

Having a good relationship with the teacher who dealt with the casuals was a great advantage. It helped them greatly if I could let them know in advance if I was not available.

Getting a block was good. For a little while, you got back to being the permanent teacher. The permanent teacher had to lay down what they wanted, and then you were on your own. I had blocks of a week, a month, and even an entire term; in one case, it was six months. I always accepted blocks in my subject areas.

A big problem with being a casual was that you often didn't know the names of the students. Another problem was learning the geography of the school. Fortunately, some schools supplied their casuals with a map. Playground duty was also a problem, once again because I didn't know the names. Sometimes, I had to tell a student to pick up some rubbish he had dropped, only to have him run away, and I was left with no option because I didn't know his name.

It was good to get back into the classroom and hone the skills that were not being used every day. I have met some of the students I taught on a casual basis, and they commented that they were pleased with my teaching.

16

Dream On

For much of my teaching life and in my retirement, I have had nightmares about teaching. I still have them occasionally, but I don't have them very often. I wake up with vivid memories of what happened. The nightmares usually fall into a few different categories:

Dream 1. Late to class. The bell rings for the start of a period, and I am caught unprepared. I fuss about, collecting my materials for the lesson, and arrive up to ten minutes after the starting time.

I have always hated doing this. When I was a deputy principal, it was sometimes inevitable. I would be caught in an interview with a parent or dealing with a student. I used to think (and still do) that deputy principals should not teach. They have far too much to do.

Dream 2. Lesson not prepared. I am on time but have to wing it.

Even up to my last days of teaching, I carried a daybook with all the lessons covered. Sometimes, the preparation consisted of few words such as "Ch. 23, Set 23.3, p. 76" or "$v = u + at$".

Dream 3. I can't find the room. I am in a new or unfamiliar school or even one which is in the process of being built, with classes going on nevertheless.

In my casual days, I was sometimes caught with not knowing where the next lesson was scheduled. I would sometimes go to the wrong room before realizing my mistake. This inevitable made me late, something I hated to be.

Dream 4. Someone, maybe a fellow teacher, has borrowed my textbook or has misplaced my notes. There has been a meeting in my staffroom, and some teacher has shifted my materials.

I did share a staffroom with one particular teacher who seemed to believe that textbooks were common property. If he couldn't see his own textbook, he would borrow one from a colleague's desk. Things got to the point where we prominently labelled all of our textbooks with our own names. If they went missing, we would look on his desk. You may recall this teacher from a previous chapter

Dream 5. I lost a battle with a student. He put one over me, and I am after retribution.

Teachers don't always win with students, and I was no exception. I find this type of nightmare very worrying because I was never in the habit of trying to extract retribution from any student. In real life, I felt embarrassed and uncomfortable, but that was all.

I guess that if psychologists or psychiatrists read this, they will try to psychoanalyse me. I hate the nightmares, but they don't occur all that often, and I don't think that I need medical help.

Epilogue

What do I have to say about those fifty-six years?

I miss the job, but I have filled in my time writing books of Physics questions and exercises. I also wrote this book. I have always hoped that my teaching has helped some young people on their journey through life, even inspiring some. I know that my decision to become a teacher of Science and Mathematics was due to the inspiration of some of my teachers. Teaching is a difficult job, and not every student at university studying for their teaching degree will survive.

I must initially thank my parents for the confidence they had in me. Going to a Catholic school was quite expensive. There was no state aid. Without hesitation, they supported me, allowing me to have a second go at the leaving certificate. Not only were they up for the fees, they had to feed and clothe me. I must give my initial thanks to my parents.

I could not have accomplished even a quarter of my life as a teacher without the support of my late wife. Every night, I brought work home. Instead having nights of conversation and mutual living, I was marking, preparing work, and so on. She never said anything about this. I spent several weeks and days away from home, not able to help her. Normally, I would bathe the children and put them to bed after dinner, either reading them stories or making up stories, but when I travelled for schoolwork, these chores fell to my wife. She supported me through years of university study. Here, I must mention her mother, who lived in a granny flat attached to our house. During the winter months, she vacated her flat during the day so that I could use it to study, which I did at a card table in the sunshine. I owe her a great deal.

After our children had all gone to school, I urged my wife to take up university studies or do something that interested her. I was quite prepared to support her. She did take up a job eventually, becoming a secretary in our local Catholic high school. She held this position for the next sixteen years, eventually retiring when it became too arduous for her. My wife even supported me when I decided to study for a master's degree after I retired. I think she was happy with her life with me. I owe all my successes to her. I know that she still helps me from Heaven.

Teaching has changed vastly, mainly for the better. When I started, teachers had little technical support. They used methods left over from the nineteenth century and were generally overworked.

Teachers of today are still overworked, and in my opinion, the job is too hard. Frequent changes of policies and syllabus requirements mean that teachers are flat out keeping up. They are given little support and very little time to develop their skills. The amount of paperwork is becoming a burden. Even to conduct a simple test requires aims, expected outcomes, and so on. Too much responsibility is being heaped onto the shoulders of teachers.

Yet, I am pleased and proud of my years as a teacher. I believe that I accomplished the very thing I wanted to do when I became a teacher: I was able to influence a lot of children, hopefully for the better. I love children, something, I believe, every teacher must be able to do.

I believe that I was instrumental in the development of many good citizens of this great country where we live; in the words of one of my last students as a permanent teacher, I taught some of them to think.

Teaching is a hard job. It is easy to become emotionally involved when dealing with children. To be a good teacher, you have to love children. They can let you down at times. At other times, they can pick you up and can do such amazing things. I became a Science teacher because I admired my Physics teacher and wanted to emulate him. Teachers, if they are good, inspire some of their "clients" to do better things. Although it is hard, teaching is a most worthwhile occupation, very essential these days, and a most satisfying profession. If you love children, you will probably do the right thing. If you give of yourself, students will respond. I was asked if I ever had an affair while I was married. I guess I did. I was in love with teaching.

I recommend it to you.

PS. Recently, I attended a function at our local high school. The principal pointed out the many wonderful things that are going on in her school. She said that the children at school today are being prepared for jobs which do not yet exist. She spoke about changes in the curriculum and new subjects which have come on board. Education today has come a long way since I began teaching. The changes are all child-centred, and that is a good thing. I wish today's teachers all the best and pray that today's students will be good citizens of the future.

Printed in the United States
By Bookmasters